FITZGERALD

v.

NITA & WESTERN RAILROAD

Wrongful Death

CASE FILE

NATIONAL INSTITUTE FOR TRIAL ADVOCACY

EDITORIAL ADVISORY BOARD

Patricia C. Bobb
Patricia C. Bobb Associates
Chicago, Illinois

Kenneth S. Broun
Professor of Law
University of North Carolina School of Law
Chapel Hill, North Carolina

Hon. Jim R. Carrigan
United States District Court
Denver, Colorado

James E. Coleman, Jr.
Carrington, Coleman, Sloman & Blumenthal
Dallas, Texas

Jacob D. Fuchsberg
Fuchsberg & Fuchsberg
New York, New York

Willie L. Leftwich
Leftwich, Moore & Douglas
Washington, D.C.

FITZGERALD

v.

NITA & WESTERN RAILROAD

Wrongful Death

CASE FILE

Laurence M. Rose
Professor of Law
University of Kansas
School of Law

National Institute For Trial Advocacy

© 1987

by

THE NATIONAL INSTITUTE FOR TRIAL ADVOCACY, INC.

PRINTED IN THE UNITED STATES OF AMERICA
ALL RIGHTS RESERVED

These materials, or any parts or portions thereof, may not be reproduced in any form, written or mechanical, or be programmed into any electronic storage or retrieval system without the express written permission of the National Institute for Trial Advocacy.

Copies of these materials are available from the National Institute for Trial Advocacy. Please direct inquiries to:

> John R. Kouris, Chief Operating Officer
> National Institute for Trial Advocacy
> Notre Dame Law School
> Notre Dame, Indiana 46556
> (800) 225-6482
> FAX (219) 282-1263

Rose, Laurence M., _Fitzgerald v. Nita & Western Railroad_, Case File, 1st Ed. (NITA, 1987).

8/94

ISBN 1-55681-114-4

ACKNOWLEDGMENTS

I express my appreciation to John Cotton, Esq. of Gaines, Mullen, Pansing, Hogan & Cotton, Omaha, Nebraska, and Richard McLeod, Esq. of Shook, Hardy & Bacon, Kansas City, Missouri, for their assistance in providing materials and transcripts upon which some of the facts for this case file have been based. The assistance of Professor Gerald Olson of the University of Missouri-Kansas City, Missouri, is also acknowledged for the development of the testimony regarding the economic impact to the estate. I wish to extend my appreciation to Professor Gary Mason of the University of Kansas for his valuable assistance in the production of the photographs used in this case file.

I also wish to express my gratitude to the University of Kansas, its School of Law and Dean Michael J. Davis for support of my work on this project during my sabbatical leave.

Lastly, I wish to thank Professor Stanley Davis of the University of Kansas School of Law, Professor Anthony Bocchino of the Temple University School of Law and Professor James Seckinger of the Notre Dame Law School for their guidance and review of the final draft of this case file.

I dedicate this case file to Pat, Josh, and Michael, whose support has allowed me to complete this project.

FITZGERALD

v.

NITA & WESTERN RAILROAD

FIRST EDITION

TABLE OF CONTENTS

	Page
INTRODUCTION	1
INSTRUCTIONS FOR USE	3
PLEADINGS	
Complaint	5
Answer	9
DEPOSITION OF DEBRA FITZGERALD	11
FUNERAL BILL	17
DEPOSITION OF ETHEL KAY	19
LETTER TO NEWSPAPER	23
TRANSCRIPT OF RECORDED STATEMENT OF STACY BECK	25
Diagram of Stacy Beck	29
POLICE REPORT	31
Diagrams	33
Photographs	35
MEMORANDUM TO PLAINTIFFS' ATTORNEY	69
REPORT OF DAVID JONATHAN & ASSOCIATES	73
Resume of David Jonathan	77
STATE OF NITA LETTER TO PLAINTIFFS' ATTORNEY	79
DOUGLAS COUNTY LETTER TO PLAINTIFFS' ATTORNEY	83

REPORT OF HARVEY GELBER, Ph.D.	85
Statement for Services of Harvey Gelber	109
Resume of Harvey Gelber	111
INCIDENT REPORT OF PAT ROMBACH	113
Statement of Steve Smolen	117
Statement of Matt Green	119
Supplement to Incident Report	121
Photographs	123
Statement of Matt Green	155
MEMORANDUM TO DEFENSE ATTORNEYS FROM PAT ROMBACH	157
Photographs	159
DEPOSITION OF CAROL BUTTERFIELD	177
DEPOSITION OF PAUL BUTTERFIELD	181
DEPOSITION OF JERI BUTTERFIELD	185
DEPOSITION OF NICK BARON	187
REPORT OF JOSHUA ALAN	189
Curriculum Vita of Joshua Alan	193
DEPOSITION OF STEVE SMOLEN	195
MEMORANDUM TO DEFENSE ATTORNEYS	197
NITA STATUTES	199
JURY INSTRUCTIONS	203
VERDICT FORM	209

INTRODUCTION

<u>Fitzgerald v. Nita & Western Railroad</u> is a wrongful death action arising out of an accident at a railroad crossing. The accident took place on October 20, YR-2, at about 5:47 p.m. at CROSSING #74647C, which is at the intersection of County Road and the main line tracks of the Nita and Western Railroad. The weather was clear and visibility was good.

The plaintiffs are the Estate of Johnny Fitzgerald and his surviving family. They contend that the railroad was negligent in not providing adequate warnings at the crossing and in the operation of the train.

The defendant contends that Johnny Fitzgerald was negligent in the operation of his car or intentionally drove his car into the train.

Discovery has been completed and each side has disclosed to the other all information that is in this casefile, including memoranda to counsel and photographs.

All years in these materials are stated in the following form:

- <u>YR-0</u>   indicates the actual year in which you are trying the actual case (i.e., the present year);

- <u>YR-1</u>   indicates the next preceding year (please use <u>the actual year</u>);

- <u>YR-2</u>   indicates the second preceding year (please use <u>the actual year</u>); etc.

INSTRUCTIONS FOR USE

Issues for Trial

This case file may be used for a trial on the issue of liability only, or on both the issues of liability and damages. If used solely for the issue of liability, the proposed jury instructions should be modified accordingly by deleting instructions 21 and 22, modifying the verdict form and deleting the testimony of the plaintiff's economist.

Witnesses

When this case file is used for a full trial, the following witnesses are available to the parties:

Plaintiff	Defendant
Debra Fitzgerald	Pat Rombach
Stacy Beck	Steve Smolen
Michael Benjamin	Carol Butterfield
David Jonathan	Joshua Alan
Harvey Gelber	

A party need not call all of the witnesses listed as its witnesses. Any or all of the witnesses may be called by either party, subject to the limitation that neither party may call more than five witnesses. If a witness is to be called by a party other than the one for whom he/she is listed, the party for whom the witness is listed will select and prepare the witness.

The following witnesses may appear by deposition only, and can be introduced by either party:

Ethel Kay — Debi Mo—
Matt Green — Broken—
Paul Butterfield — Carol husband
Jeri Butterfield — Paul Mom's
Nick Baron

Required Stipulations

1. The statements made in the edited depositions are admissible to the same extent as statements from full depositions.

2. Nita City is a fairly large city. Approximately 30 miles to the southeast is the rural town of Wellington

(pop. 15,000). Marion is at the far southwest corner of the state of Nita, approximately 250 miles from Wellington.

   3.   Rich April no longer works for Nita & Western Railroad and cannot be located.

   4.   The letters from the state of Nita (page 79) and Douglas County (page 83) are authentic.

IN THE CIRCUIT COURT OF
DOUGLAS COUNTY, NITA
CIVIL DIVISION

DEBRA FITZGERALD,)
Administratrix of the Estate)
of JOHNNY FITZGERALD, and)
DEBRA FITZGERALD, individually)
and on behalf of her minor child)
CARRIE FITZGERALD)
)
Plaintiffs) COMPLAINT
)
vs.)
)
NITA & WESTERN RAILROAD CO.)
)
Defendant)

Plaintiffs for their complaint against Defendant allege:

1. At all times material, plaintiffs are and were residents of Wellington, Douglas County, Nita.

2. Plaintiff Debra Fitzgerald was appointed Administratrix of the Estate of Johnny Fitzgerald by the Probate Court of Douglas County, Nita on November 15, YR-2 and is the widow of Johnny Fitzgerald; Carrie Fitzgerald is the daughter of Johnny Fitzgerald and Debra Fitzgerald.

3. Defendant Nita & Western Railroad Co. is a corporation organized and existing under the laws of the State of Nita, with a principal place of business in Nita City, Nita.

4. On October 20, YR-2, at approximately 5:47 p.m., Johnny Fitzgerald was operating an automobile on County Road in Douglas County, Nita in an easterly direction, approaching railroad crossing #74647C.

5. At this time and place, defendant, acting through its agents and employees, was operating a freight train in a northerly direction on railroad tracks belonging to the defendant.

6. At the intersection of said road and tracks, the vehicle operated by Johnny Fitzgerald was in a collision with the train operated by the defendant and, as a result

of the collision, Johnny Fitzgerald suffered severe injuries which caused his death.

7. The collision and resulting death of Johnny Fitzgerald was solely caused by the negligence of the defendant in failing to adequately and timely warn Johnny Fitzgerald of the oncoming train, in operating the train at a unsafe speed and in failing to maintain a proper lookout.

8. Prior to his death, Johnny Fitzgerald was a healthy individual, capable of and supporting his wife and minor child. As a result of his death, Debra Fitzgerald and Carrie Fitzgerald have been deprived of:

(a) The reasonably expected net income of Johnny Fitzgerald;

(b) Services, protection, care and assistance of Johnny Fitzgerald, whether voluntary or obligatory;

(c) Society, companionship, comfort, guidance, kindly offices and advice of Johnny Fitzgerald.

9. As a result of his death, the Estate of Johnny Fitzgerald has incurred reasonable funeral and burial expenses in the amount of $2500.00.

Wherefore, Plaintiffs demand judgment against the defendant, Nita & Western Railroad Co. in the amount of $1,000,000, together with interest thereon, costs of this action and for such other relief as the Court deems just and proper.

Plaintiffs demand trial by jury in this action.

DEBRA FITZGERALD,

By *Thomas Busch*
Thomas Busch
Attorney for Plaintiffs
2000 Johnson Drive
Wellington, Nita

Dated: December 12, YR-2

Return of Summons

I hereby certify that the above complaint was personally served on James Bell, President and authorized process agent for Nita & Western Railroad Co.

_____
James Brown
Process Server

Dated: December 15, YR-2

IN THE CIRCUIT COURT OF
DOUGLAS COUNTY, NITA
CIVIL DIVISION

DEBRA FITZGERALD,   )
Administratrix of the Estate)
of JOHNNY FITZGERALD, and   )
DEBRA FITZGERALD, individually)
and on behalf of her minor child)
CARRIE FITZGERALD   )
)
            Plaintiffs   )   ANSWER
)
vs.   )
)
NITA & WESTERN RAILROAD CO.)
)
            Defendant   )

Defendant for its answer to the Plaintiffs' complaint:

1. Admits the allegations contained in paragraphs 1-6.

2. Denies the allegations of paragraph 7.

3. Is without sufficient knowledge or information to form a belief as to the truth of the allegations of paragraphs 8 and 9, and therefore denies them.

AFFIRMATIVE DEFENSES

4. Any injuries sustained or suffered by Johnny Fitzgerald at the time and place mentioned in the Plaintiffs' complaint (and therefore any resulting injuries suffered by Plaintiffs) were caused in whole or in part, or were contributed to, by the negligence and/or intentional act of Johnny Fitzgerald and not by any negligence on the part of defendant.

Wherefore, Defendant requests that judgment be entered in its favor in this action, together with costs of this action and for such other relief as the Court deems just and proper.

Defendant demands trial by jury.

                        NITA & WESTERN RAILROAD CO.

                        By _/s/ John Cotton_____
                           John Cotton
                           Cotton & McLeod
                           Regency Plaza, Suite 1300
                           Nita City, Nita

Dated: December 22, YR-2

Certificate of Service

I hereby certify that on December 22, YR-2, a copy of the above Answer was placed in the United States mail, postage prepaid, addressed to Thomas Busch, Attorney for the Plaintiff, 2000 Johnson Drive, Wellington, Nita.

                                         _/s/ John Cotton_____
                                         John Cotton
                                         Cotton & McLeod

DEPOSITION OF DEBRA FITZGERALD*
MARCH 16, YR-1

My name is Debra Fitzgerald, but everyone calls me Debi. I am 23 years old. I was born on November 19, YR-25 in Nita City. I live at 16 Meadowbrook Lane in Wellington, Nita with my daughter, Carrie, who was born on May 22, YR-7. I am the widow of Johnny Fitzgerald, who died on October 20, YR-2, four days short of his 25th birthday.

I grew up in Nita City and lived with my parents, Ethel and Irv Kay throughout high school. I attended Nita City High but did not finish. Johnny and I were married at my parents' home in Nita City on January 3, YR-7. I received my general degree by correspondence after I got married and went to City Tech for some secretarial courses after Carrie was 18 months old. I hope to become a secretary as soon as I finish school. I expect to go back to City Tech as soon as I get enough money. At the time of my husband's death, I was working the 4 to 8 p.m. shift at the Flinders Aluminum Plant, helping in the stockroom with inventory. My job was temporary for the fall. I always tried to have some extra money for special things. I usually worked the late afternoons so that Johnny could watch Carrie when he came home from work. He worked the seven to three shift at the new Uprite Scaffolding plant as a welder. At the time of his death he was earning approximately $280 per week. Johnny's income went to pay all of the bills for the house, food and all. My paycheck was for extra things and for presents, such as the new shotgun I had bought as a surprise present for Johnny's birthday, but didn't get a chance to give to him. We didn't have a lot of money in the bank, but we were comfortable.

We were a very happy family. Johnny and I were best friends and always had a great time together. We cared for each other a great deal and hardly ever fought. Johnny was devoted to Carrie. He would always read to her at night and take long walks with her before dinner. He was especially good to her and was always taking her with him on trips to the supermarket, the library and department stores for presents for birthdays and holidays. As a matter of fact, Johnny had taken Carrie to buy a new costume for Halloween, and my dad had to take her out on Halloween because I just

---

*The transcript of Debra Fitzgerald's deposition was excerpted so that only her answers are reprinted here. Assume that this is a true and accurate rendering of those answers.

DEPOSITION OF: DEBRA FITZGERALD
DATE: MARCH 16, YR-1

couldn't do it. Carrie really missed her dad that night. She still does.

We spent a lot of time with my parents. Johnny and my dad did a lot of work renovating the den at my parents' home. He loved to work with his hands and help people. He was just that type of person. At the time of his death, Johnny was in good health and so were the rest of us. He was enjoying his job, and had just received his five year pin for being with Uprite. He was looking forward to his ten year pin, and had recently talked about the retirement benefits which he had just become entitled to.

Johnny also enjoyed his high school friends from Wellington High, especially his best friend Paul Butterfield. Johnny was the best man at Paul's wedding on July 4, YR-3. We spent a lot of time with Johnny's friends whenever they came home. We even went camping with some of them sometimes. I really didn't care for camping much, but because Johnny liked it we went together. Since Johnny's friends were mostly guys, I became friends with their girlfriends or wives. I knew that Johnny was friendly with all of them before we started dating, but I was never considered an outsider. Johnny and Carol Butterfield (his friend Paul's wife) had dated each other before we were married, but had broken up just before Johnny and I started dating. They continued to be very friendly and sometimes I was concerned about their relationship. During a camping trip with Paul and Carol about a year before they got married, I saw Johnny and Carol talking very quietly while Paul and I were cooking dinner. Later that evening, Johnny had told me that Carol had asked him to take her for a walk where they could be alone, so they could make love. I was shocked and told Johnny that I wanted to go home immediately, but Johnny said not to worry, that she was just fooling around and probably wasn't serious. Even if she was, Johnny said, he was in love with me and Carrie and didn't want anything to affect our wonderful family. After that night, I just couldn't get real close to Carol. I was always thinking that she felt I took Johnny away from her and that she married Paul just to stay close to Johnny.

On Saturday, October 19, the day before he died, we went to visit Paul and Carol Butterfield, who had come to stay with Paul's mother, Jeri. The Butterfields had come to Wellington to help celebrate the birthday of George

DEPOSITION OF DEBRA FITZGERALD
DATE: MARCH 16, YR-1

Carlisle, a friend of Paul and Johnny from high school. Since Carol and Paul lived in Marion, we only got to see them a few times a year. They brought their new baby girl, Shelly and we hadn't see the baby yet. We had gotten to Mrs. Butterfield's house about 5:30. We expected to stay over and sleep in the downstairs guest room. The guys, Johnny, Paul and their friends George and Richard played pool downstairs while Carol, the baby, Carrie and I stayed upstairs with Paul's mother. The children played while we watched TV. At about 8:00, the guys went out to have dinner and some beer while we got the children ready for bed. Carol needed some diapers for the baby, so I went with her in her car to the store. We got back in about 20 minutes, at about 9:10, fed the baby and put the children to sleep. About 9:30 Carol and I went to meet the guys at Rocco's. We had 2-3 beers while we were there, danced to the music and had a pretty good time. Johnny danced with Carol and I danced with Paul for one dance and then Johnny and Carol talked a little in the corner booth. When Johnny came back. I asked him what they talked about, and he said that Carol wanted to know what she should buy Johnny for his birthday. We stayed until about 10:45 when Carol had to go home to nurse the baby. While she was feeding the baby, I checked on Carrie, who was asleep, and then watched TV alone. At about 12:00, Johnny and Paul came home. Paul was feeling the effects of the beer and Johnny had to help him into the house. After getting Paul into his room, Johnny said he wanted to go home rather than stay over, so I collected Carrie and our things and Johnny drove us home. Johnny appeared to be in good spirits and said that he expected that Paul would sleep late, so there was no reason to stay overnight. Johnny did not have a lot to drink and drove home carefully. As a matter of fact Johnny did not like to drink.

On the day he died, Carrie and I woke up late, after Johnny was already up. I was still tired from getting home late from visiting the Butterfields. After breakfast, Johnny and Carrie went for a walk. About 10:00, I called Carol and Paul to thank them for the night before. Paul was still sleeping, so I told Carol to have Paul call Johnny later to say goodbye before they left. When Johnny and Carrie came back I told him that I was going to take Carrie to Nita City to visit my parents, do some laundry and maybe go to a movie since he wanted to watch the football games on TV. I didn't really say when we would be home. Johnny left to get a newspaper about 12:00 and I left about 12:30 to go to my parents'.

DEPOSITION OF: DEBRA FITZGERALD
DATE: MARCH 16, YR-1

We got there about 1:15, brought in my laundry, which was in an overnight case, and talked for a while. Then I took Carrie to a movie. We got back about 4:30 and helped with dinner. After dinner, my dad took Carrie for a walk. Around 7:00, I got a call from Carol looking for Johnny so they could say goodbye. I said that he wasn't with me at my parents' house, that he was at home, but maybe he went out for a pizza. I told Carol that we would see her the next time they visited and hung up the phone. Then I left Carrie with my parents and went to the laundromat. The first I knew about the accident was about 7:30 p.m. My mom came into the laundromat and told me that that Johnny had been killed by a train. I fainted and had to go to into the hospital for a few days because I was in shock. The funeral was shortly after that, but I really don't remember much about it. I was in a fog during the whole time. Carrie and I got some help in handling the house after Johnny died, and his company's life insurance money has kept us going. It will run out soon and I hope to get a job as soon as I can finish my secretarial training. Right now I have to take care of Carrie. She misses her daddy very much. Some friends have been very helpful, especially Linda Roth and Chuck Reynolds. Chuck was my supervisor at the Flinders Aluminum plant and we have become very close friends. He has been extremely good to Carrie.

The accident occurred about 8 or 9 miles from where we live. I don't think that Johnny had ever been on that road before, but I can't be sure. The road leads to the new Uprite plant, but Johnny usually took the main road to get to work. I know this because I sometimes drove Johnny to work and he said that the main road was faster and shorter from our house. He had hunted in the general area of the plant before it was built and maybe he had gone out there to find a place for hunting. Pheasant season began on October 28 and I know that Paul and Johnny had made plans to go hunting.

Johnny's car was a YR-7 Ford, but it was in good shape. Johnny did all the work on it himself to save money. About two weeks before the accident, he had a problem with his brakes and did a whole brake job on the car. In fact Johnny also tuned up the engine and adjusted all of the hoses and things in preparation for the winter. I don't think that anything went wrong with the car. Johnny was a careful driver, too. He never went too fast, although he did not

DEPOSITION OF: DEBRA FITZGERALD
DATE: MARCH 16, YR-1

always stay within the speed limit. No one really does. The only reason that this accident occurred that makes any sense is that the railroad did something wrong.

No, Johnny and I had never talked about a separation, divorce or anything like that. We were a very happy couple.

I have read this deposition and the answers are correct to the best of my knowledge and belief.

Debra Fitzgerald
Debra Fitzgerald

Harold Dench
Notary Public

Fitzgerald Case File

```
                    ERICKSON'S MORTUARY
                       12 Main Street
                      Wellington, Nita
```

Debra Fitzgerald
16 Meadowbrook Lane
Wellington, Nita

                            STATEMENT

For Services Rendered:

      Transportation, October 20, YR-2
      Preparation and Chapel, October 20-23, YR-2
      Transportation and Burial, October 23, YR-2

              $2500.00

Payment Received November 27, YR-2 by *Melissa Ryan*
                                               Erickson's Mortuary

DEPOSITION OF ETHEL KAY*
APRIL 15, YR-1

My name is Ethel Kay and I am 55 years old. I live at 211 Bluebell in Nita City with my husband Irv. My daughter is Debra Fitzgerald. She is my only child.

Debra is a fine girl and she is a very good mother to Carrie, my granddaughter. Debi was a good student in high school and received good grades. She was never a problem to us when she was growing up. In high school she got to be very friendly with a group of people in Wellington, where we had a summer house. I really didn't care for the people there, but they were nice to us. She dated a little while we were down there, but nothing serious until the fall of YR-8 when she began to date Johnny Fitzgerald. He was a nice boy although not like the boys Debi dated from Nita City. We didn't disapprove of him but we didn't really encourage her either. In late December, Debi and Johnny came to us and told us that Debi was pregnant. Needless to say, we were upset but felt we had to support our little girl. We quickly arranged a wedding and they were married in our home on January 3, YR-7. Carrie was born that May 22.

Debi and Johnny were happy and they both loved their daughter. I never knew them to fight or argue and they have always loved to spend time with each other. Johnny was a good provider and worked hard. He loved to work with his hands and always helped us around the house, even helping my husband finish our den. Johnny and Debi spent a lot of time with us and they had a bedroom in our house so that they could stay over anytime. Both of them came to see us whenever both were in Nita City and sometimes one or the other would come up to spend time. While Johnny was working or hunting, Debi might visit and when Debi was working, Johnny might bring Carrie for dinner. It was a very happy situation.

On Sunday, October 20, YR-2, Debi called to say that she and Carrie were coming up for the day. Debi wanted to take Carrie to a movie in the afternoon and then do some laundry. Johnny was going to watch the football game on TV. She arrived at our house about 1:15 and brought her laundry in a suitcase into the house. Debi and Carrie visited for a

---

*The transcript of Ethel Kay's deposition was excerpted so that only her answers are reprinted here. Assume that this is a true and accurate rendering of those answers.

DEPOSITION OF: ETHEL KAY
DATE: APRIL 15, YR-1

while and then went to the movies. They came back about 4:30 and helped me prepare dinner. We had our dinner and Carrie and my husband went out for a walk about 6:00 and came back right after sunset. At about 7:00, the phone rang and Debi answered it. She talked for about two minutes and hung up the phone. I asked who it was and she said it was the Butterfields who were looking for Johnny to say goodbye. Debi and Johnny had spent the day with the Butterfields on Saturday and Paul and Carol were going back to Marion, early the next morning. Debi wondered where Johnny might be, since they said they had tried to call him at home, but Debi felt he might have gone out to get something to eat.

At about 7:15, Debi left to go to the laundromat. About 5 minutes later, we got a phone call from Chief Neely of the Wellington Police Department. He said that he had heard some bad news over the radio and felt that we needed to know. He said that Johnny had been killed at a railroad crossing. I was in shock. I told my husband and he told me to go to the laundromat to get Debi while he stayed with Carrie. I went to the laundromat and told Debi the bad news. She fainted and I had to call an ambulance to take her to the hospital. She stayed there until Tuesday, and we watched Carrie and made the funeral arrangements. The funeral was Wednesday, but Debi was in a fog for about a week.

We have been very supportive of Debi and Carrie. She has tried to make it by herself financially, but I know it is going to be hard without some help. She has some good friends who help her emotionally. She has asked us not to give her money, only moral support. We try the best we can. For example, my husband helped by taking Carrie out on Halloween, just like her daddy was going to do.

About a week after the funeral, I wrote a letter to the editor of the Wellington newspaper about the accident and the negligence of the railroad. I am amazed by the lack of care of the railroad in not putting automatic flashing lights in all of their crossings. My lawyer told me that this was gross negligence and I asked him to recommend a lawyer in Wellington. I gave the name to Debi and she contacted him. He is the one who filed this lawsuit.

Around the first of April, I received a phone call from Jeri Butterfield, Paul's mother. She said that her daughter-in-law, Carol, had been asked to and gave a deposition in

DEPOSITION OF: ETHEL KAY
DATE: APRIL 15, YR-1

the case and was concerned about what was going on in the case. She said that Carol didn't want to hurt Debi or Carrie and I told her that if Carol wanted to help she should just stay out of it. Carol was always sticking her nose into Debi and Johnny's business. I really think that she was jealous of the happiness that Johnny and Debi had together.

No, Debi never talked of leaving Johnny. Why would she say anything about that? They were very happy together. Who is saying that they were separating? No, Debi did not bring any clothes with her that night other than her laundry and they were not planning to stay over that night. Where are you getting this from?

I have read this deposition and the answers are correct to the best of of my knowledge and belief.

Ethel Kay
Ethel Kay
April 15, YR-1

Harold Dench
Notary Public

WELLINGTON DAILY JOURNAL-NEWS, NOVEMBER 2, YR-2

LETTER TO THE EDITOR

Dear Editor:

Something has to be done about the reckless actions of the Nita & Western Railroad in maintaining the railroad crossings in Wellington. They continually disregard the rights of innocent people when they do not upgrade crossings and install automatic safety signals at crossings which have increased traffic and lead to populated areas. Just two weeks ago my daughter lost her husband when he was run over and killed by a freight train that went through an uncontrolled crossing without taking proper precautions. Crossings like the one on County Road must be protected by flashing lights and bells to protect everyone. If the railroad doesn't begin to think of someone else besides themselves then other people will die.

Mrs. Ethel Kay
Mrs. Ethel Kay
Nita City

N ↑

My house →

Kitchen
Dining Room
Living Room
Entry + Porch
Bathroom
Laundry
Bedroom

← 100 feet →

100 feet

County Road

Stacy Beck
11/23/YR-2

-29-
Fitzgerald Case File

INVESTIGATOR'S MOTOR VEHICLE ACCIDENT REPORT

TOTAL NUMBER OF VEHICLES INVOLVED: 2

DATE OF ACCIDENT: Month 10, Day 20, Year YR-2
DAY OF ACCIDENT: SAT (x)
TIME OF ACCIDENT: 1747 HRS
MILITARY TIME
FOR STATE USE ONLY

PLACE WHERE ACCIDENT OCCURRED:
- COUNTY: DOUGLAS
- CITY, TOWN OR TOWNSHIP: WELLINGTON
- ACCIDENT OCCURRED ON PRIVATE PROPERTY: [ ]

ROAD ON WHICH ACCIDENT OCCURRED: COUNTY ROAD
POSTED SPEED LIMIT: 50

DISTANCE FROM MILEPOST: (blank)

IF NOT AT INTERSECTION: Railroad Crossing #74647C

IF ACCIDENT WAS OUTSIDE CITY LIMITS, INDICATE DISTANCE FROM NEAREST TOWN: 1.5 MILES W of Wellington

---

VEHICLE-1

DRIVER: Johnny Fitzgerald
DRIVER'S ADDRESS: 16 Meadowbrook, Wellington, NT
DRIVER'S LICENSE: DOB 10/24/-27, NT, W3F1R4, NT, MALE
LICENSE PLATE: YR-1, NT, DGF-459
ESTIMATED DAMAGE TO VEHICLE: 2000 TOTAL
VEHICLE: Year YR-7, Make Ford, Model Sedan, Body Style 2-DR, Color Black
VIN: OK91U22135
ODOMETER READING: Unknown
OWNER: SAME
OWNER'S ADDRESS: SAME

VEHICLE-2

DRIVER: Steve Smolen
DRIVER'S ADDRESS: 449 Clearmeadow, Nita City, NT
DRIVER'S LICENSE: DOB 6/25/-40, N/A, MALE
LICENSE PLATE: N/A
ESTIMATED DAMAGE TO VEHICLE: 500
VEHICLE: Year YR-22, Make GM, Model GP7, Body Style Locomotive
VIN: 1563
OWNER: Nita & Western Railroad
OWNER'S ADDRESS: Nita City, NT

RESTRAINT INFORMATION

VEHICLE-1: 2
VEHICLE-2: N/A

Codes: 1. Not available 2. Lap belt 3. Lap and shoulder 4. Child restraint 5. Passive restraint 6. Not in use 7. Unknown

---

THIS SECTION IS FOR INFORMATION ON INJURED PERSONS ONLY

NAME: Johnny Fitzgerald
AGE: 25
ADDRESS: 16 Meadowbrook, Wellington, NT
VEHICLE NUMBER: 1
SEX: Male
SEATING POSITION: 4
INJURIES: Crushed Skull
TAKEN TO: Erickson's Mortuary
BY WHOM: Erickson's Mortuary
EJECTION: Yes
TYPE OF INJURY: Fatal injury

WITNESSES

NAME	ADDRESS	PHONE
Rich April	Route 7, Nita City, NT	
Matt Green	716 Main, Nita City, NT	
Stacy Beck	Route 8, Wellington, NT	

DR Form 40, Nov 84 — 1810

-31-
Fitzgerald Case File

THE FOLLOWING INFORMATION IS REQUIRED FOR ALL ACCIDENTS

DRIVER AND VEHICLE INFORMATION

VEHICLE MOVEMENT BEFORE COLLISION

	N	S	E	W	ROAD OR HIGHWAY NAME
1			■		County Rd
2	■				RR TRacks

VEH (1, 2)
1. ■ ☐ Going ahead
2. ☐ ☐ Passing
3. ☐ ☐ Turning right
4. ☐ ☐ Turning left
5. ☐ ☐ Making "U" turn
6. ☐ ☐ Slowing down
7. ☐ ☐ Starting in traffic lane
8. ☐ ☐ Starting from parked position
9. ☐ ☐ Backing up
10. ☐ ☐ Stopped in traffic lane
11. ☐ ☐ Parked
12. ☐ ☐ Merging
13. ☐ ☐ Changing lanes

DISPOSITION OF VEHICLE (Check one per vehicle)

VEH 1 / VEH 2
1. ☐ ☐ Towed away
2. ☐ ☐ Abandoned
3. ☐ ☐ Driven away
4. ☐ ☐ Unknown

VEHICLE-1
13. ☐ TOP
14. ☐ BOTTOM
15. ☐ TOTAL
16. ☐ UNKNOWN

VEHICLE-2
13. ☐ TOP
14. ☐ BOTTOM
15. ☐ TOTAL
16. ☐ UNKNOWN

VEHICLE CONDITION (Check one per vehicle)

VEH 1 / VEH 2
1. ☐ ☐ No defects
2. ☐ ☐ Defective Brakes
3. ☐ ☐ Defective lights
4. ☐ ☐ Defective signals
5. ☐ ☐ Defective steering
6. ☐ ☐ Defective tires
7. ■ ☐ Unknown
8. ☐ ☐ Other (Specify)

MAJOR REASON FOR NOT SEEING DANGER (Check one per vehicle)

VEH 1 / VEH 2
1. ☐ ☐ None
2. ☐ ☐ Rain, snow, ice on windshield
3. ☐ ☐ Dirty windshield
4. ☐ ☐ Trees, crops, etc.
5. ☐ ☐ Buildings
6. ☐ ☐ Embankment
7. ☐ ☐ Traffic sign
8. ☐ ☐ Billboard
9. ☐ ☐ Parked vehicle
10. ☐ ☐ Moving vehicle
11. ■ ☐ Other (Specify)

MAJOR CONTRIBUTING CIRCUMSTANCES (Check one per accident)

VEH 1 / VEH 2
1. ☐ ☐ Speed too fast for conditions
2. ☐ ☐ Exceeding speed limit
3. ☐ ☐ Alcohol or drugs
4. ☐ ☐ Failure to yield
5. ☐ ☐ Drove left of center
6. ☐ ☐ Improper overtaking
7. ☐ ☐ Ran stop sign
8. ☐ ☐ Disregarded traffic signal
9. ☐ ☐ Following too closely
10. ☐ ☐
11. ☐ ☐ Made improper turn
12. ☐ ☐ Improper or no turn signal
15. ☐ ☐ Evasive action
16. ☐ ☐ Backing unsafely
18. ■ ☐ Other (Specify below)
19. ☐ ☐ Improper lane change
20. ☐ ☐ Animal on roadway

Inattentiveness

DRIVER'S CONDITION (Check one per vehicle)

VEH 1 / VEH 2
1. ■ ☐ Normal
2. ☐ ☐ Asleep
3. ☐ ☐ Illness
4. ☐ ☐ Fatigue
5. ☐ ☐ Drinking
6. ☐ ☐ Unknown
7. ☐ ☐ Other (Specify)

PEDESTRIAN'S CONDITION (Check one)
1. ☐ Normal
2. ☐ Asleep
3. ☐ Illness
4. ☐ Fatigue
5. ☐ Drinking
6. ☐ Unknown
7. ☐ Other (Specify)

ACCIDENT INFORMATION

ROAD CHARACTER (Check one)
1. ☐ Straight and level
2. ■ Straight and on grade
3. ☐ Straight and at hillcrest
4. ☐ Curved and level
5. ☐ Curved and on grade
6. ☐ Curved and on hillcrest

ROAD TYPE (Check one)
1. ☐ One lane
2. ■ Two lanes
3. ☐ Three lanes
4. ☐ Four or more lanes
5. ☐ Divided roadway
6. ☐ Interstate

ROAD SURFACE (Check one)
1. ☐ Concrete
2. ■ Black top
3. ☐ Brick
4. ☐ Gravel
5. ☐ Dirt
6. ☐ Other (Specify)

ROAD SURFACE CONDITION (Check one)
1. ■ Dry
2. ☐ Wet
3. ☐ Snowy - icy
4. ☐ Other (Specify)

WEATHER (Check one)
1. ■ Clear
2. ☐ Raining
3. ☐ Snowing
4. ☐ Fog
5. ☐ Cloudy
6. ☐ Other (Specify)

Temperature

PEDESTRIAN'S ACTION (Check one)
1. ☐ Crossing at intersection - with signal
2. ☐ Crossing at intersection - against signal
3. ☐ Crossing at intersection - no signal
4. ☐ Crossing - not at intersection
5. ☐ Walking with traffic
6. ☐ Walking against traffic
7. ☐ Standing in roadway
8. ☐ Getting on or off other vehicle
9. ☐ Working on vehicle on roadway
10. ☐ Other working in roadway
11. ☐ Playing in roadway
12. ☐ Other in roadway
13. ☐ Not in roadway
14. ☐ Other (Specify)

ROAD WORK (Check one)
1. ☐ Construction zone
2. ☐ Maintenance activity
3. ☐ Not applicable

TRAFFIC CONTROL (Check up to two)
1. ☐ None
2. ☐ Stop sign
3. ☐ Yield sign
4. ☐ Traffic signal
5. ☐ Pedestrian signal
6. ☐ Pedestrian crosswalk
7. ☐ Flashing beacon
8. ☐ Railroad warning sign
9. ■ Railroad crossing sign
10. ☐ Railroad flashing beacon
11. ☐ Railroad gates & signal
13. ☐ Officer/flagman
14. ☐ No passing zone (signs)
15. ☐ No passing zone (paint stripes)
16. ☐ Other (Specify)

LIGHT CONDITION (Check one)
1. ■ Daylight
2. ☐ Dawn - dusk
3. ☐ Darkness
4. ☐ Darkness - streetlights on
5. ☐ Darkness - streetlights off

INDICATE BY DIAGRAM WHAT HAPPENED

See Attached Diagrams

N ↑

Narrative: Vehicle #1 was eastbound on County Road when it collided with rear of first box car on freight train. Vehicle #1 apparently struck box car #1 just in front of rear wheels and was dragged by train along tracks. Box car #1 ran over vehicle #1, causing back wheels to derail and break coupling between box car #1 and box car #2. Train continued along tracks with rear section stopping, Vehicle #1 being pulled along and then stopping, then front part of train stopping. No vissible signs of skid marks at scene, only scuff marks at collision site. Conclusion that there was no attempt to stop Vehicle #1.

Engineer of train said "We were northbound and unaware of anything until the train went into emergency." Pat Rombach, investigator for railroad, advised that speed tape in engine showed train was traveling at 48 mph at time of accident. Train consisted of four engines and 85 cars (24 loaded, 61 empty) with total weight of 4033 tons. Crossing protected by one crossbuck sign facing east on north side of road.

Inattentiveness was probably the major cause of the accident.

DESCRIBE BELOW WHAT HAPPENED: (Refer to vehicle by number)

Should location have engineering study	☐ YES ■ NO	Were photographs taken	■ YES ☐ NO	Was investigation made at scene ■ YES ☐ NO
Is investigation complete ■ YES ☐ NO		Driver report form furnished to	☐ 1 ☐ 2	

INVESTIGATOR'S RANK & WRITTEN SIGNATURE:	DEPARTMENT:	OFFICER NO.	TROOP:	MO.	DAY	YR.
Michael Benjamin, Trooper	Nita State Police	122	C	10	22	-2

MAIL TO: ACCIDENT RECORDS BUREAU, DEPARTMENT OF ROADS

Fitzgerald Case File

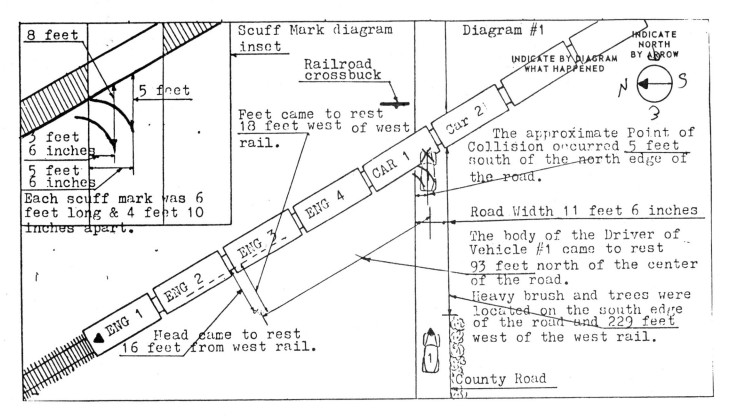

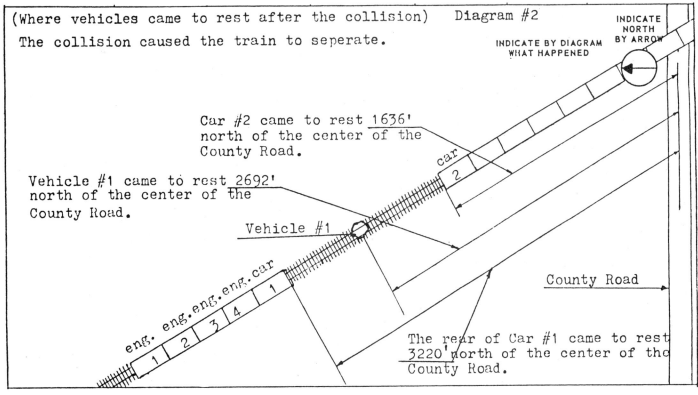

-33-
Fitzgerald Case File

Fitzgerald Case File

Fitzgerald Case File

Photo #6

Fitzgerald Case File

Photo #7

Fitzgerald Case File

Fitzgerald Case File

Photo #9

Fitzgerald Case File

Fitzgerald Case File

Photo #13

Fitzgerald Case File

MEMORANDUM

TO: Tom Busch, Attorney
FROM: Laura Fine, Paralegal
DATE: January 19, YR-1
SUBJECT: Fitzgerald v. Nita & Western RR

At your request, I today interviewed State Trooper Mike Benjamin regarding his investigation of the accident involving our client's husband, Johnny Fitzgerald, and the N&W freight train on October 20, YR-2. I was especially concerned about the description of the photographs he took. The substance of the interview follows.

Trooper Mike Benjamin, DOB 1/22/YR-25, is a graduate of Lisle High School and received an associate degree in administration of criminal justice from Columbia County Community College in YR-5. He then joined the Nita State Police. In connection with his training as a trooper he has attended the State Police Training Academy in Nita City for two months including a two-week session on accident investigation, as well as another two-week session put on by the Northwestern Traffic Institute in Evanston, Illinois. Over the last five years he has investigated over 500 automobile accidents, but this was the first auto-train collision he had investigated.

He was on routine patrol on Sunday, October 20, YR-2, when he received a call to report to County Road at the railroad crossing to investigate an accident. He approached the intersection from the west and did not observe any advance warning sign that a railroad crossing was coming up. He arrived at the scene at about 6:00 pm and found the train in two sections with the railroad employees examining the train. One of the railroad men indicated that he had found a man up the tracks and Benjamin went to the location. He found Mr. Fitzgerald, determined that he was dead and observed that Mr. Fitzgerald had suffered a crushed skull. He covered the body and then radioed to cancel the ambulance and request the mortuary/coroner to come out. He spoke to the railroad investigator who arrived shortly thereafter and began taking measurements with the aid of a passer-by. He took the names of the railroad witnesses as well as the neighbor who was on the scene and who told him that he had called the police but had not been an eyewitness.

He told me that he noticed two definite scuff marks near the tracks, just west of the rails, that were fresh. He was unable to say on the basis of the physical evidence exactly where the train had been separated, but was fairly confident that it had separated as a result of going over the car which it had dragged.

He also confirmed that there was only one crossbuck, that it was facing east with lettering on the east side, and that it was in disrepair in that one of the cross pieces was broken.

He took two sets of photographs. The first set was at about 6:25 in the evening the night of the accident, just after sunset. The second set was on the following day at about 2:30 pm. He is not very familiar with the crossing and could not comment about any level of traffic across the tracks, nor of any recent increases.

Photo 1 shows the grooves from the rear wheels of the Fitzgerald car and its relationship to the tracks. Also shown is the box car that stopped at the crossing. Photo 2 shows the front section of the train with the derailed wheels on box car #1 and the four engines. It was taken from east of the tracks looking northwesterly. Photo 3 is of box car #1 and the front of the train. Clearly shown are the scrape marks on the rear portion of box car #1 where the car impacted. Photo 4 shows the derailed wheels on box car #1. Photo 5 shows the Fitzgerald car where it came to rest.

All of the remaining photos were taken the next day. Photo 6 was taken from the top of the hill west of the crossing, looking easterly. It is the beginning of a steep incline and the tracks are pictured in the distance. Photo 7 is going down the incline with the tracks still visible. Photo 8 is farther down the road with the tracks no longer visible. Photo 9 is yet farther down the road; the tracks are still not visible. Photo 10 is again down the road. Photo 11 is at the bottom of the incline. Photo 12 is at a point 325 feet west of the crossing looking east toward the tracks, which now become visible. Photo 13 is from the 325 foot point and looking through the brush and trees towards the southwest where the train was coming from; it was taken from eye level from inside the trooper's car. Photo 14 is taken from a point 250 feet south of the crossing down the tracks looking northwest to the point where the car is 325 feet up the road; the car is barely visible. Photo 15 is again looking east from the road at the 275 foot mark; the crossbuck is barely visible. Photo 16 is looking east at the 225 foot mark; the crossbuck is now clearly visible. Photo 17 is from the previously noted point on the tracks (250 south of the center line of the street) looking northwest with the car at the 225 foot mark.

Trooper Benjamin was also clear that it was the railroad's obligation to keep the brush down along the road for a reasonable distance. Although the roadside foliage may have blocked Fitzgerald's view of the train, Benjamin felt that the whistle should have warned him of the oncoming train. While Fitzgerald was in the darkness of the foliage and broke out into the light, Benjamin felt that there was still enough time to see the train and stop. He was apparently unaware that the whistle was not sounding and I did not mention this fact to him.

[Margin note: Ask him how long it takes to stop at 50mph]

I asked him if he had any theory why there were no skid marks. He indicated that there could only be two causes: intentional and unintentional. If it was unintentional, it was the result of inattention. If it was intentional, he either committed suicide or there was a malfunction of the car and Fitzgerald tried to beat the train across the crossing. He will make a convincing witness as to the photos, although we must counter his conclusion as to the inattentiveness of our decedent.

David Jonathan & Associates, Inc.
19 Erin Marie Court
Nita City, Nita

Consultants in Railroad Safety
and Engineering

December 15, YR-1

Thomas Busch, Esq.
2000 Johnson Drive
Wellington, Nita

RE: Nita & Western Railroad
Crossing #74647C
County Road
Wellington, Nita

Dear Mr. Busch:

In accordance with your request, I have conducted an examination concerning the above crossing and the accident of October 20, YR-2. Based upon my investigation, it is my opinion that Nita & Western Railroad was negligent in the following ways:

1. Failure to timely upgrade the crossing to include flashing signals and audible warnings;

2. Failure of the engineer to sound whistles to warn nearby traffic;

3. Failure of the engineer to light the headlamp of the lead engine during operation;

4. Failure to maintain a clearly visible railroad crossing.

In connection with my investigation, I have examined the following documents:

1. State Police Report concerning the accident, with photos, dated October 22, YR-2;

2. Available Maps;

3. Report of Pat Rombach, Investigator for Nita & Western Railroad, with photographs, dated October 26, YR-2;

4. Letter to you from Nita Highway and Transportation Commission, dated Nov. 30, YR-1 with attached hourly traffic count for period Feb. 26-Mar. 4, YR-2;

5. Letter to you from Douglas County Highway Department, dated Nov. 22, YR-1;

6. Letter to John Cotton, Esq. from Dr. Joshua Alan, dated May 21, YR-1.

In addition, I visited the actual crossing on two occasions. The first was on October 24, YR-1, four days after the first anniversary of the accident and again on December 1, YR-1.

Although the history of this crossing shows only one automobile-train accident during the last 25 years, the increased traffic resulting from the establishment of the new Uprite scaffolding plant (occupied September, YR-3) leads me to conclude, in my expert opinion, that automatic flashing/sounding signals should have been installed long before this accident. In fact, they should have been installed as soon as a full crew was operating to build the plant. For the entire time I was with the Louisville & Nashville and Union Pacific, the standard procedure at those railroads and in the industry today is that as soon as the state highway commission puts a crossing on an eligibility list for flashing light signals, within two weeks the railroad's engineering crew would do a feasibilty study on whether automatic signals should be installed at that crossing. Included in this feasibility study would not only be a study of present traffic conditions, but also a study of conditions which could be anticipated in the following six months based on local construction or predictable traffic patterns. Based on the data supplied by the state that this crossing was placed on an eligibility list in March, YR-2, and the fact that the traffic to the plant was increasing, the Nita & Western was negligent in either not doing the study or in not installing the automatic crossing signals called for by the study within a timely manner. Doing a feasibility study 11 months after placement on the eligibility list and installation of flashing lights 17 months after the placement are both acts of negligence, although taking 6 months for the installation is reasonable.

Since I have worked in railroads for over 45 years, I am well aware of standard railroad regulations regarding requirements for headlamps and whistles. By state law and railroad regulations, whistles must be sounded at least 1200 feet in advance of a railroad crossing and the front headlamp of the lead engine must be burning at all times, day or night, with minor exceptions. These are necessary

-74-
Fitzgerald Case File

safety procedures which, if not followed, make it materially more difficult for an automobile driver to see or hear a train approaching a crossing. In my expert opinion, having examined the scene and the photographs taken on the day of the accident, if the light was not burning and the whistle not sounding, it would be extremely difficult for Mr. Fitzgerald, in diminishing daylight and breaking out of an area of dense foliage, to observe the train at the crossing.

As to the extent of the foliage, I believe that the railroad could certainly have made clearer the approach to the intersection. I would suggest based upon the speed limit of the road, that all dense foliage should have been cleared 350 feet from the crossing.

Furthermore, I agree with Dr. Joshua Alan that the marks at the crossing were not skid marks, but were caused by the train pulling the car. Accordingly, it is apparent that Mr. Fitzgerald was not alerted by any sound or light. Therefore, the whistle was not sounding and the headlamp was not lit.

To date I have spent 8 hours on this matter. Accordingly, please treat this letter as an invoice for $1000.00. Should you require my services for a deposition or for in-court testimony, please advise me as soon as possible so that no scheduling differences arise.

Very truly yours,

David Jonathan

David Jonathan, President
David Jonathan & Associates, Inc.

RESUME

DAVID JONATHAN

ADDRESS: 19 Erin Marie Court
Nita City, Nita

Age: 67

EDUCATION:

B.S., Civil Engineering
University of Nita
May, YR-45

EMPLOYMENT:

President
David Jonathan & Associates, Inc.
Consultants specializing in railroad safety and engineering
YR-5 to Present

Chief Civil Engineer
Union Pacific Railroad
YR-35 to YR-5

Staff Engineer
Louisville and Nashville Railroad
YR-45 to YR-35

EXPERT WITNESS EXPERIENCE:

Testimony for both plaintiffs and defendants
Qualified as an expert in 4 federal and 3 state courts
Testified in-court in 12 cases on:
- crossing safety
- operations safety
- civil engineering

FEES:

$125.00 per hour for investigation and report
$125.00 per hour for deposition preparation/testimony
$100.00 per hour for in-court preparation/testimony
Reimbursement of all necessary expenses

STATE OF NITA
HIGHWAY AND TRANSPORTATION COMMISSION
State Office Building
Nita City, Nita

Theresa DeSalvo, Chairman

November 30, YR-1

Thomas Busch, Esq.
2000 Johnson Drive
Wellington, Nita

RE: Nita & Western
Crossing #74647C
County Road
Wellington, Nita

Dear Mr. Busch:

Reference is made to your letter of November 2, YR-1, concerning the subject crossing. A review of our files indicates that only one vehicle count was taken at this location during the last five years. A copy of the summary sheet for the count which occurred from February 26 to March 4, YR-2, is enclosed.

Regarding your request for a priority list, please be advised that we have an ongoing program to upgrade railroad crossings. In conjunction with this program, we develop a number of eligibility listings which are constantly changing as conditions in the field change. Once a crossing appears on an eligibility listing, the railroad is required, within a reasonable time, to do a feasibility study to determine what, if any, crossing upgrade work is merited. The crossing in question first appeared on an eligibility listing in March of YR-2. Our records show that a feasibility study was done by N & W in February, YR-1 and that flashing light signals were installed at the crossing in August of YR-1.

If we may be of any additional assistance, please advise.

Very truly yours,

Robert Oliver
Chief Engineer

Location Number: 861   Direction: Both   Year: YR-2

Crossing: 74647C   County Road   Douglas County

Nita & Western Railroad

Period: Feb. 26, 10:30 a.m. through March 4, 8:30 a.m.

	Thur Feb 26 AM	Thur Feb 26 PM	Fri Feb 27 AM	Fri Feb 27 PM	Sat Feb 28 AM	Sat Feb 28 PM
1		13	4	21	10	28
2		38	2	41	1	28
3		54		50	1	48
4		88	5	74	2	33
5		74	16	59	2	24
6		41	47	55	17	37
7		26	61	33	17	24
8		17	35	20	25	25
9		18	16	19	31	16
10		12	13	18	46	9
11	28	7	26	21	41	7
12	26	6	24	15	32	12

	Sun Mar 1 AM	Sun Mar 1 PM	Mon Mar 2 AM	Mon Mar 2 PM	Tues Mar 3 AM	Tues Mar 3 PM	Wed Mar 4 AM
1	7	24		11	2	18	2
2	8	32		18	2	29	3
3	3	49	1	42	1	51	
4	2	44	1	78	3	74	3
5	1	23	12	56	13	58	15
6	2	32	41	92	43	46	40
7	3	19	52	24	50	27	51
8	12	17	20	19	20	11	33
9	27	13	23	17	22	20	
10	26	11	23	17	10	10	
11	28	6	10	9	22	8	
12	38	2	24	7	24	8	

Totals		24 hours	Avg./hr	6am-10pm	Avg./hr
Thur	Feb 26	448	32.000	435	36.250
Fri	Feb 27	675	28.125	565	35.313
Sat	Feb 28	516	21.500	464	29.000
Sun	Mar 1	429	17.875	398	24.875
Mon	Mar 2	597	24.875	526	32.875
Tue	Mar 3	572	23.833	492	30.750
Wed	Mar 4	147	18.375	84	42.000

DOUGLAS COUNTY
STATE OF NITA
HIGHWAY DEPARTMENT

205 North Second Street
Wellington, Nita

November 22, YR-1

Thomas Busch, Esq.
2000 Johnson Drive
Wellington, Nita

RE: Nita & Western Railroad
Crossing #74647C
County Road, Wellington, Nita

Dear Mr. Busch:

In response to your letter of November 2, YR-1 requesting traffic counts at the crossing referred above, the following is the traffic count information we have available.

   1. YR-2 traffic count by the State of Nita - average daily traffic 620.

   2. Traffic count by Douglas County in March/April, YR-1 average daily traffic 1089.

I hope that the above information is useful.

Sincerely,

Stanley Davis
Stanley Davis
County Highway Engineer

ECONOMIC ANALYSIS REPORT
RE: JOHNNY FITZGERALD

Prepared by:

HARVEY GELBER

Professor of Economics
University of Nita
Nita City, Nita

June 10, YR-1

Basic Facts:

Johnny Fitzgerald, a white male, was born on October 24, YR-27, in Wellington, Nita. He was educated through high school and began his employment life immediately thereafter with the Uprite Scaffolding Company, continuing with Uprite until his death. He married Debra Fitzgerald on January 3, YR-7. A daughter, Carrie, was born on May 22, YR-7. There was a history of a good family life and work history. There was regular advancement in salary and responsibilities at employment.

Mr. Fitzgerald died in a car-train accident on October 20, YR-2. At the time of his death, he was a welder earning $280.00 for a normal 40 hour week (annualized to $14,560.00) and received standard fringe benefits.

Source: Deposition of Debra Fitzgerald

Summary of Loss:

The following summarizes the estimated loss of the survivors of Johnny Fitzgerald, namely his wife, Debra, and his daughter, Carrie.

Loss of Wages (Exhibit A).	$416,771
Loss of Fringe Benefits (Exhibit A)	85,980
Total Compensation Loss	$502,751
Add: Value of Household Services	80,423
Gross Loss	$583,174
Less: Personal Consumption	159,163
Net Loss	$424,011

Discussion:

1. Prior to his death, Johnny Fitzgerald's normal life expectancy was to age 72.8. Source: U.S. National Center for Health Statistics, Vital Statistics of the U.S.; (Exhibit B).

2. Annual wages of $14,560 was projected forward until a retirement age of 65 at 5.4% per year. This is conservative, as a later retirement might be taken based upon the character of Mr. Fitzgerald. The 5.4% rate represents the historic (1947-1985) average rate of wage increase for production workers in sheet metal manufacturing plants. Source:

computed from data appearing in U.S. Dept. of Labor, <u>Employment & Earnings, 1909-84</u> and June, 1986 Supplement. (Exhibits C and D).

3. Fringe benefits included private pension, social security, health insurance, unemployment and workers compensation insurance. These fringe benefits have a value nationwide equal to 20.63% of gross wages and is computed as follows:

Workers compensation	1.5%
Unemployment	1.3
Retirement	3.7
Health insurance	4.4 Total 10.9%

Gross wages is 84% divided by 10.9% is 12.98% of gross
          add social security   7.65%
          Total fringe   20.63%

This rate was assumed to remain constant throughout Mr. Fitzgerald's employment. Source: computed from date in U.S. Dept. of Labor, <u>Handbook of Labor Statistics, 1980.</u> (Exhibit E).

4. All fringe benefits and wages were reduced by the normal probability of unemployment for white males. These probabilities, by age group, are:

25-34	3.5%
35-44	2.7%
45-54	2.9%
55-64	3.4%

These are historic averages and are computed from data in U.S. Dept. of <u>Labor, Handbook of Labor Statistics, 1985</u> at Table 27.

5. Services performed around the house by family members have an economic value. For a male with similar circumstances to Mr. Fitzgerald, these services have an annual value, in 1979 dollars, depending upon the age of family members and size of family as follows:

Age		
25-29	$1500	(Child age 6-11)
30-36	2400	(Child age 12-17)
37-39	1900	(No children)
40-54	1100	
55-65	1500	
66-73	2700	(Wife retired)

Source: Cornell University study, 1980. (Exhibit F). This does not include the services value to people outside the immediate family. These values were projected forward at 5.88% per year, the historic rate of increase in the price of domestic services, 1947-1977. Source: computed from information in U.S. Dept. of Labor, Handbook of Labor Statistics 1978. (Exhibits G and H).

6. Because Mr. Fitzgerald would have consumed a portion of his income, this would not be available to the survivors. It must be subtracted from gross loss. Depending upon age and number of family members, Mr. Fitzgerald's consumption varies over his lifetime from 35% to 40% of his income. Source: computed from U.S. Dept. of Labor, Bulletin 1570-2, Revised Equivalence Scale. (Exhibit I).

7. All values after January, YR-0, were discounted to present value at 7.5%, a reasonable average rate on a portfolio of essentially risk-free U.S. Government securities. This rate only pertains to present market conditions; it will change if market interest conditions change. If interest rates increase, salary growth will likely increase, and the discounted values will remain essentially unchanged. Inflation is not considered as a factor in these computations as it will not affect the discount rate.

COMPUTER OUTPUT: LOSS OF WAGES AND FRINGE BENEFITS

YR	WAGES	FRIN	TOTAL	PRES VALUE FACTOR	EMPL FACTOR	ADJ PRES VALUE WAGES	ADJ PRES VALUE FRING
-2	2912	601	3513	1	.965	2810	580
-1	15346	3166	18512	1	.965	14809	3055
0	16175	3337	19512	.9302326	.965	14520	2995
+1	17048	3517	20565	.8653326	.965	14236	2937
+2	17969	3707	21676	.8049606	.965	13958	2880
+3	18939	3907	22846	.7488005	.965	13685	2823
+4	19962	4118	24080	.6965586	.965	13418	2768
+5	21040	4340	25380	.6479615	.965	13156	2714
+6	22176	4575	26751	.6027549	.965	12899	2661
+7	23373	4822	28195	.5607022	.965	12647	2609
+8	24635	5082	29718	.5215835	.973	12503	2579
+9	25966	5357	31323	.4851939	.973	12258	2529
+10	27368	5646	33014	.4513432	.973	12019	2479
+11	28846	5951	34797	.4198541	.973	11784	2431
+12	30403	6272	36676	.3905620	.973	11554	2384
+13	32045	6611	38656	.3633135	.973	11328	2337
+14	33776	6948	40744	.3379660	.973	11107	2291
+15	35600	7344	42944	.3143870	.973	10890	2247
+16	37522	7741	45263	.2924530	.973	10677	2203
+17	39548	8159	47707	.2720493	.973	10469	2160
+18	41684	8599	50283	.2530691	.971	10243	2113
+19	43935	9064	52998	.2354131	.971	10043	2072
+20	46307	9553	55860	.2189890	.971	9847	2031
+21	48808	10069	58877	.2037107	.971	9654	1992
+22	51443	10613	62056	.1894983	.971	9466	1953
+23	54221	11186	65407	.1762775	.971	9281	1915
+24	57149	11790	68939	.1639791	.971	9100	1877
+25	60235	12427	72662	.1525387	.971	8922	1841
+26	63488	13098	76586	.1418964	.971	8747	1805
+27	66916	13805	80721	.1319967	.971	8577	1759
+28	70530	14550	85080	.1227876	.966	8366	1726
+29	74338	15336	89674	.1142210	.966	8202	1692
+30	78353	16164	94517	.1062521	.966	8042	1659
+31	82584	17037	99621	.0988392	.966	7885	1627
+32	87043	17957	105000	.0919434	.966	7731	1595
+33	91744	18927	110670	.0855288	.966	7580	1564
+34	96698	19949	116647	.0795616	.966	7432	1533
+35	101919	21026	122945	.0740108	.966	7287	1503
+36	107423	22161	129585	.0688473	.966	7144	1474
+37	113224	23358	136582	.0640440	.966	7005	1445
+38	95470	19696	115166	.0595758	.966	5494	1133
Tt	2024162	417585	2441746			416771	85980

EXHIBIT B

Vital Statistics

NO. 107. EXPECTATION OF LIFE AND EXPECTED DEATHS, BY RACE, AGE, AND SEX: 1979

AGE IN 1979 (years)	EXPECTATION OF LIFE IN YEARS					EXPECTED DEATHS PER 1,000 ALIVE AT SPECIFIED AGE				
	Total	White		Black		Total	White		Black	
		Male	Female	Male	Female		Male	Female	Male	Female
At birth	73.7	70.6	78.2	64.0	72.7	13.15	12.90	10.00	23.84	19
1	73.7	70.5	78.0	64.6	73.1	.88	.93	.69	1.29	1
2	72.8	69.6	77.1	63.6	72.2	.68	.68	.54	1.08	
3	71.8	68.6	76.1	62.7	71.3	.55	.53	.44	.91	
4	70.9	67.6	75.2	61.8	70.4	.45	.45	.36	.77	
5	69.9	66.7	74.2	60.8	69.4	.39	.41	.30	.66	
6	68.9	65.7	73.2	59.9	68.4	.35	.38	.27	.57	
7	68.0	64.7	72.2	58.9	67.5	.32	.36	.24	.50	
8	67.0	63.8	71.2	57.9	66.5	.28	.32	.21	.43	
9	66.0	62.8	70.3	56.9	65.5	.24	.27	.19	.38	
10	65.0	61.8	69.3	56.0	64.5	.21	.22	.18	.35	
11	64.0	60.8	68.3	55.0	63.5	.21	.22	.18	.35	
12	63.0	59.8	67.3	54.0	62.6	.26	.29	.20	.40	
13	62.1	58.8	66.3	53.0	61.6	.38	.48	.26	.51	
14	61.1	57.9	65.3	52.1	60.6	.54	.75	.33	.68	
15	60.1	56.9	64.3	51.1	59.6	.72	1.04	.42	.86	
16	59.2	56.0	63.4	50.1	58.6	.90	1.31	.50	1.06	
17	58.2	55.0	62.4	49.2	57.7	1.04	1.53	.56	1.30	
18	57.3	54.1	61.4	48.3	56.7	1.13	1.68	.58	1.57	
19	56.3	53.2	60.5	47.3	55.7	1.19	1.76	.59	1.86	
20	55.4	52.3	59.5	46.4	54.8	1.24	1.83	.58	2.16	
21	54.5	51.4	58.5	45.5	53.8	1.30	1.89	.58	2.47	
22	53.6	50.5	57.6	44.7	52.9	1.33	1.93	.58	2.74	
23	52.6	49.6	56.6	43.8	51.9	1.35	1.91	.58	2.99	
24	51.7	48.7	55.6	42.9	51.0	1.34	1.86	.58	3.20	
25	50.8	47.8	54.7	42.1	50.0	1.33	1.80	.58	3.41	
26	49.8	46.9	53.7	41.2	49.1	1.32	1.74	.59	3.62	
27	48.9	46.0	52.7	40.4	48.1	1.30	1.68	.59	3.79	
28	48.0	45.1	51.8	39.5	47.2	1.30	1.64	.60	3.90	
29	47.0	44.1	50.8	38.7	46.3	1.29	1.60	.62	3.98	
30	46.1	43.2	49.8	37.9	45.3	1.29	1.58	.64	4.05	
31	45.2	42.3	48.9	37.0	44.4	1.30	1.56	.67	4.14	
32	44.2	41.3	47.9	36.2	43.5	1.33	1.57	.70	4.24	
33	43.3	40.4	46.9	35.3	42.5	1.38	1.59	.75	4.38	
34	42.3	39.5	46.0	34.5	41.6	1.44	1.65	.81	4.54	
35	41.4	38.5	45.0	33.7	40.7	1.53	1.72	.87	4.72	
36	40.5	37.6	44.1	32.9	39.8	1.62	1.82	.95	4.91	
37	39.5	36.7	43.1	32.0	38.9	1.74	1.94	1.04	5.17	
38	38.6	35.8	42.1	31.2	38.0	1.88	2.07	1.14	5.50	
39	37.7	34.8	41.2	30.4	37.1	2.03	2.24	1.26	5.89	
40	36.8	33.9	40.2	29.6	36.2	2.21	2.43	1.38	6.34	
41	35.8	33.0	39.3	28.8	35.3	2.42	2.65	1.53	6.80	
42	34.9	32.1	38.4	28.0	34.4	2.64	2.92	1.68	7.21	
43	34.0	31.2	37.4	27.3	33.6	2.89	3.22	1.85	7.56	
44	33.1	30.3	36.5	26.5	32.7	3.17	3.58	2.04	7.88	
45	32.2	29.4	35.6	25.8	31.9	3.46	3.96	2.23	8.19	
46	31.4	28.5	34.7	25.0	31.0	3.78	4.38	2.45	8.57	
47	30.5	27.7	33.7	24.3	30.2	4.15	4.83	2.70	9.08	
48	29.6	26.8	32.8	23.5	29.4	4.55	5.34	2.97	9.75	
49	28.8	26.0	31.9	22.8	28.6	4.99	5.88	3.27	10.55	
50	27.9	25.1	31.0	22.1	27.8	5.47	6.48	3.60	11.40	
51	27.1	24.3	30.2	21.4	27.0	5.98	7.11	3.95	12.24	
52	26.3	23.5	29.3	20.7	26.2	6.48	7.74	4.30	13.05	
53	25.5	22.7	28.4	20.1	25.5	6.98	8.37	4.65	13.82	
54	24.7	21.9	27.6	19.4	24.7	7.49	9.01	5.02	14.56	
55	23.9	21.2	26.7	18.8	24.0	8.00	9.66	5.39	15.24	
56	23.1	20.4	25.9	18.2	23.2	8.55	10.36	5.80	15.92	
57	22.3	19.6	25.0	17.6	22.5	9.23	11.22	6.30	16.66	
58	21.5	18.9	24.2	17.0	21.8	10.04	12.27	6.88	17.49	
59	20.8	18.2	23.4	16.5	21.1	10.96	13.45	7.55	18.34	
60	20.0	17.5	22.6	15.9	20.4	11.96	14.70	8.27	19.28	
61	19.3	16.8	21.8	15.4	19.8	12.93	15.93	9.01	20.11	
62	18.6	16.1	21.0	14.9	19.1	13.82	17.08	9.70	20.54	
63	17.9	15.5	20.2	14.4	18.5	14.55	18.12	10.30	20.43	
64	17.3	14.8	19.5	13.9	17.9	15.19	19.06	10.85	19.97	
65	16.6	14.2	18.7	13.3	17.2	15.81	19.97	11.44	19.32	
70	13.4	11.3	15.0	10.7	13.9	20.38	25.05	15.82	21.78	
75	10.6	8.8	11.7	8.6	11.5	27.04	30.03	24.07	27.11	
80	8.4	6.9	9.0	7.8	10.7	30.71	30.56	32.13	23.64	
85 and over	6.7	5.5	7.0	6.8	9.2	269.17	177.73	376.75	115.63	

Source: U.S. National Center for Health Statistics, *Vital Statistics of the United States*, annual.

-93-
Fitzgerald Case File

U.S. Dept. of Labor, Employment & Earnings, Manufacturing 1909-84

EXHIBIT C

SIC 3444 — SHEET METAL WORK (Con.)

WOMEN EMPLOYEES — IN THOUSANDS

Year	Ann. Avg.	Jan.	Feb.	Mar.	Apr.	May	June	July	Aug.	Sept.	Oct.	Nov.	Dec.
1958	5.0	4.6	4.9	4.9	4.5								
1959		4.8			5.1	5.1	5.2	5.3	5.1	5.0	4.8	4.9	5.0
1960	5.1	4.8	5.0	5.0	5.1	5.2	5.2	5.2	5.2	5.2	5.3	5.1	5.1
1961	5.3	4.9	5.1	5.1	5.2	5.4	5.5	5.4	5.4	5.4	5.4	5.3	5.3
1962	5.4	5.0	5.2	5.1	5.4	5.4	5.5	5.4	5.5	5.5	5.4	5.3	5.2
1963	5.6	5.1	5.2	5.2	5.5	5.6	5.7	5.6	5.9	6.0	5.8	5.7	5.8
1964	6.2	5.9	6.0	6.0	6.1	6.3	6.4	6.4	6.3	6.4	6.3	6.1	6.2
1965	6.7	6.3	6.4	6.4	6.5	6.6	6.6	6.6	7.1	6.9	6.8	7.1	7.2
1966	7.9	7.1	7.3	7.4	7.5	7.9	8.0	8.1	8.2	8.2	8.3	8.4	8.3
1967	8.5	8.2	8.3	8.2	8.3	8.3	8.6	8.6	8.6	8.6	8.7	8.8	8.8
1968	9.3	8.8	8.9	8.9	9.0	9.3	9.5	9.5	9.3	9.5	9.6	9.7	9.6
1969	10.0	9.5	9.3	9.7	9.7	9.8	10.1	10.0	10.3	10.2	10.4	10.7	10.6
1970	10.2	10.4	10.2	10.2	10.2	10.3	10.3	10.4	10.3	10.2	10.1	9.8	9.6
1971	9.5	9.6	9.6	9.1	9.0	9.2	9.6	9.7	9.7	9.7	9.6	9.5	9.4
1972	9.7	9.3	9.4	9.4	9.4	11.0	9.8	11.1	11.3	11.1	10.9	10.0	10.1
1973	11.0	10.3	10.6	10.7	10.8	11.0	11.8	11.8	11.4	11.4	11.4	11.2	11.2
1974	11.2	11.0	11.0	11.3	10.8	12.0	11.8	11.8	11.4	11.2	10.9	10.6	10.1
1975	10.4	9.9	11.0	10.7	10.2	10.7	10.7	10.7	10.5	10.5	10.9	10.6	10.1
1976	11.2	10.5	11.0	10.8	11.1	11.4	11.7	11.6	11.5	11.3	11.2	11.6	11.6
1977	12.3	11.5	11.4	11.8	11.9	12.2	12.1	12.2	12.5	12.8	12.9	13.0	13.3
1978	14.6	13.4	13.6	13.9	14.3	14.5	14.7	14.5	14.8	14.9	15.3	15.4	15.4
1979	16.3	15.4	15.7	15.7	15.9	16.0	16.3	16.3	16.4	16.6	17.0	17.1	16.9
1980	15.7	16.7	16.5	16.6	16.2	15.7	15.3	15.3	15.4	15.3	15.5	15.2	15.1
1981	15.4	15.2	15.3	15.4	15.6	15.6	15.6	15.4	15.4	15.4	15.4	15.0	14.9
1982	14.3	14.5	14.3	14.5	14.5	14.3	14.2	14.2	14.1	14.4	14.4	14.4	14.2
1983	15.0	14.0	14.2	14.1	14.3	14.7	14.9	15.3	15.5	15.3	14.4	15.3	14.2
1984		15.9	16.3	16.6	16.8	16.9	17.3	17.5	15.5	15.6	15.8	15.9	15.9

PRODUCTION WORKERS — IN THOUSANDS

Year	Ann. Avg.	Jan.	Feb.	Mar.	Apr.	May	June	July	Aug.	Sept.	Oct.	Nov.	Dec.
1958	36.9	35.9	34.8	34.6	34.7	35.5	36.7	37.0	38.8	39.7	39.1	38.3	37.2
1959	40.1	36.6	36.9	38.1	40.1	41.0	43.8	44.1	41.4	40.0	39.1	39.6	40.4
1960	41.8	40.0	39.8	39.4	40.2	42.0	43.4	42.9	44.2	44.1	43.4	41.4	40.4
1961	41.8	38.1	38.7	39.2	40.4	41.5	43.1	43.6	44.0	44.1	43.7	43.3	42.1
1962	42.7	40.2	40.3	40.5	42.1	43.2	44.1	44.0	44.9	44.4	43.8	42.7	41.9
1963	43.7	41.2	41.2	41.1	42.7	43.7	44.9	44.8	46.1	46.4	45.4	44.3	43.1
1964	45.0	41.9	42.5	43.2	43.8	44.2	45.7	46.1	47.0	47.1	46.0	46.0	46.0
1965	48.9	45.4	45.8	46.3	46.5	48.5	49.9	51.0	51.2	51.4	49.7	50.1	50.5
1966	54.2	50.2	50.8	51.9	52.4	53.8	55.7	57.4	56.8	55.6	55.5	55.0	55.1
1967	54.9	54.4	54.0	53.9	54.1	54.3	57.1	56.3	55.9	54.6	54.3	54.8	54.8
1968	57.3	53.9	54.1	55.1	55.4	56.4	58.1	58.0	58.1	59.5	59.8	59.4	59.4
1969	60.6	58.6	59.1	59.3	59.8	60.0	62.1	61.3	62.4	61.0	60.9	61.1	61.2
1970	59.9	60.3	59.9	60.0	59.0	58.1	61.0	61.1	62.0	61.9	59.6	58.2	56.8
1971	60.0	56.3	57.7	57.4	57.9	58.6	61.3	61.1	62.0	62.9	63.2	62.6	60.9
1972	63.0	61.0	60.5	59.5	60.7	62.1	63.1	63.7	64.1	64.9	65.4	65.5	65.0
1973	68.4	64.5	65.3	65.8	66.7	67.3	70.2	69.7	70.5	68.9	70.1	69.5	69.8
1974	69.3	68.9	68.8	69.8	70.7	71.0	72.6	71.7	70.7	68.9	68.1	66.1	64.1
1975	60.1	61.6	60.0	59.3	59.0	58.9	60.3	60.1	60.7	60.9	60.4	60.3	59.4
1976	62.4	58.4	57.8	60.0	61.3	61.8	63.3	61.1	63.7	64.3	64.1	64.5	64.6
1977	65.7	64.5	64.7	66.1	67.4	68.9	70.2	62.3	70.6	73.5	73.9	74.2	73.8
1978	70.2	73.6	72.8	73.9	75.7	76.4	78.5	79.3	79.8	81.1	81.6	81.8	81.6
1979	83.1	80.5	80.7	80.5	80.2	81.4	83.9	83.6	83.8	84.2	85.5	86.2	86.7
1980	81.3	86.3	84.6	83.5	81.5	79.5	79.8	79.1	80.8	81.0	80.9	79.7	79.2

See footnotes at end of tables.

SIC 3444 — SHEET METAL WORK (Con.)

PRODUCTION WORKERS — IN THOUSANDS

Year	Ann. Avg.	Jan.	Feb.	Mar.	Apr.	May	June	July	Aug.	Sept.	Oct.	Nov.	Dec.
1981	78.3	78.4	77.4	77.5	78.2	78.2	79.4	79.5	79.5	79.2	78.7	78.0	76.0
1982	72.3	74.0	73.3	73.2	73.3	72.8	72.4	71.5	71.5	72.3	71.6	71.5	70.5
1983	74.9	69.2	69.6	69.7	70.3	72.1	74.1	75.6	77.6	79.4	80.3	80.6	79.9
1984		78.3	79.9	81.5	82.7	83.5	85.5	86.6					

PRODUCTION-WORKER AVERAGE WEEKLY EARNINGS — IN DOLLARS

Year	Ann. Avg.	Jan.	Feb.	Mar.	Apr.	May	June	July	Aug.	Sept.	Oct.	Nov.	Dec.
1947	50.93	47.04	48.24	47.80	49.32	51.34	52.16	50.79	51.57	51.73	53.10	53.17	55.43
1948	55.76	55.20	53.29	54.82	54.41	55.49	55.93	50.44	58.48	54.26	59.39	58.32	58.81
1949	56.68	58.32	57.34	56.50	54.28	57.01	56.71	57.32	56.76	57.39	54.49	57.06	57.35
1950	61.22	57.99	57.96	57.45	57.82	59.45	59.32	60.08	62.60	62.95	64.83	64.00	65.83
1951	69.46	66.02	68.15	68.23	70.56	69.55	68.71	67.54	68.95	69.77	71.80	70.00	73.68
1952	74.16	70.99	70.99	70.30	68.25	78.00	71.86	71.96	74.80	78.02	79.00	78.86	79.10
1953	79.10	77.15	78.21	78.02	79.23	78.88	77.71	74.67	78.91	81.56	82.32	79.76	79.77
1954	77.61	76.81	75.66	76.44	76.04	78.59	78.78	78.39	78.20	78.01	77.62	77.03	79.40
1955	83.64	77.03	78.01	77.79	79.00	82.60	84.02	85.68	85.08	86.11	88.62	86.74	88.20
1956	89.23	86.73	84.66	85.27	87.35	89.04	89.03	88.17	89.84	91.96	91.98	90.23	92.60
1957	92.16	89.79	90.61	90.58	89.24	91.80	89.52	93.43	93.84	93.96	92.69	91.54	94.30
1958	95.36	92.50	91.89	90.78	92.19	94.40	95.27	93.45	100.19	100.77	100.86	95.44	99.06
1959	101.02	97.04	97.53	99.06	101.11	103.66	105.33	103.25	101.02	99.31	100.86	99.20	102.16
1960	103.22	100.90	99.50	100.10	100.65	104.08	105.59	104.90	105.83	104.90	104.65	102.11	102.14
1961	105.30	102.14	101.12	102.68	102.94	103.83	105.78	106.90	106.08	107.68	109.56	106.90	106.25
1962	107.73	104.94	104.81	107.46	106.92	108.53	108.65	107.73	108.92	110.27	108.79	106.67	108.68
1963	111.25	107.73	108.13	107.46	106.65	110.57	111.38	112.06	113.42	114.39	114.63	112.46	113.71
1964	114.96	110.97	113.16	113.84	113.16	113.57	114.53	114.12	116.20	119.23	117.18	117.04	119.56
1965	119.42	116.34	116.20	123.35	116.62	120.33	126.78	117.96	126.30	119.23	121.40	125.22	123.08
1966	125.16	119.89	121.93	123.35	123.02	125.33	126.78	124.80	126.30	127.87	127.24	125.22	129.02
1967	126.79	126.07	123.12	124.53	123.97	125.97	125.97	126.48	126.30	128.52	128.84	128.11	129.02
1968	132.11	126.48	128.07	124.53	125.53	131.61	132.89	130.73	131.84	134.55	135.71	136.04	137.94
1969	143.03	137.16	136.82	138.99	141.25	142.96	145.46	143.09	143.91	146.97	147.44	144.49	151.01
1970	148.45	146.65	144.91	147.90	147.23	148.37	148.83	149.23	150.05	148.93	150.44	149.74	152.86
1971	160.80	151.31	150.54	155.61	154.05	158.40	162.81	164.43	165.22	165.21	166.46	165.21	168.44
1972	174.47	167.48	167.90	167.45	171.14	172.37	175.71	175.24	176.08	179.55	179.11	189.20	179.56
1973	184.68	186.84	178.04	183.31	180.54	183.96	175.10	185.49	186.96	189.47	190.65	202.87	189.34
1974	194.44	186.86	186.28	189.05	182.58	192.72	194.08	194.04	197.11	203.09	202.98	202.87	204.97
1975	206.56	201.76	199.68	194.82	205.13	201.49	206.06	203.90	208.74	209.43	211.92	213.79	218.90
1976	218.44	211.85	213.72	217.85	215.97	219.60	220.95	217.65	217.65	217.79	223.84	219.36	224.55
1977	232.00	216.40	222.22	226.12	223.97	227.30	233.16	232.06	235.60	238.79	241.59	239.99	243.81
1978	245.52	231.55	233.14	241.19	242.00	241.16	245.81	247.90	248.06	250.97	251.93	251.93	258.16
1979	263.74	252.41	253.44	259.60	247.94	260.83	264.27	262.36	267.13	274.00	271.32	269.68	277.78
1980	285.04	271.75	268.19	274.95	277.36	279.41	285.38	283.67	289.38	299.30	294.42	294.75	307.20
1981	319.14	301.86	299.92	310.08	308.88	315.21	318.75	320.23	326.73	325.48	330.37	331.14	342.91
1982	339.29	320.14	333.29	337.74	330.91	335.34	340.28	345.54	343.93	345.35	343.93	346.21	354.12
1983	354.71	347.77	342.14	351.12	351.39	351.74	356.31	352.91	354.32	360.00	357.29	361.09	369.36
1984		358.60	353.63	355.71	355.71	362.60	366.12	362.18					

PRODUCTION-WORKER AVERAGE HOURLY EARNINGS — IN DOLLARS

Year	Ann. Avg.	Jan.	Feb.	Mar.	Apr.	May	June	July	Aug.	Sept.	Oct.	Nov.	Dec.
1947	1.267	1.197	1.197	1.195	1.200	1.246	1.288	1.299	1.299	1.313	1.308	1.316	1.352
1948	1.401	1.343	1.339	1.357	1.350	1.370	1.381	1.405	1.444	1.447	1.470	1.458	1.452
1949	1.457	1.458	1.459	1.445	1.463	1.456	1.454	1.466	1.463	1.464	1.434	1.452	1.463
1950	1.519	1.483	1.471	1.473	1.475	1.490	1.498	1.502	1.523	1.543	1.551	1.561	1.594
1951	1.69	1.63	1.65	1.66	1.68	1.63	1.68	1.68	1.69	1.71	1.73	1.72	1.75
1952	1.80	1.74	1.74	1.74	1.75	1.76	1.77	1.79	1.82	1.84	1.85	1.86	1.87
1953	1.92	1.85	1.88	1.88	1.90	1.91	1.90	1.90	1.92	1.97	1.96	1.95	1.96

U.S. Dept. of Labor, Employment & Earnings, Supplement, June 1986

EXHIBIT D

MANUFACTURING

SIC 345

Year	Ann. Avg.	Jan.	Feb.	Mar.	Apr.	May	June	July	Aug.	Sept.	Oct.	Nov.	Dec.

SIC 3444—SHEET METAL WORK

ALL EMPLOYEES—IN THOUSANDS

1983	103.0	97.9	98.4	98.4	99.6	100.6	102.7	103.7	105.2	106.8	107.0	107.5	106.7
1984	110.8	106.0	106.3	107.4	108.3	109.0	111.5	112.4	112.8	114.1	114.6	114.2	112.5
1985	110.6	109.8	108.9	108.9	109.7	109.8	111.2	111.3	112.4	112.7	112.3	110.9	109.2
1986		108.0	107.1										

WOMEN EMPLOYEES—IN THOUSANDS

1983	14.8	14.0	14.2	14.1	14.4	14.6	14.9	15.0	15.3	15.3	15.3	15.4	15.6
1984	16.5	15.5	15.8	16.1	16.2	16.4	16.7	16.8	16.7	17.0	16.9	16.8	16.5
1985	16.2	16.3	16.0	16.0	16.3	16.4	16.5	16.5	16.5	16.2	16.1	16.0	15.8
1986		15.7	15.6										

PRODUCTION WORKERS—IN THOUSANDS

1983	73.9	69.2	69.6	69.7	70.5	71.6	73.6	74.5	76.1	77.5	77.8	78.2	78.1
1984	81.3	76.3	77.1	78.2	79.2	79.9	81.8	82.9	83.4	84.5	85.0	84.6	82.9
1985	81.5	80.7	79.4	79.6	80.6	80.8	82.1	82.0	83.0	83.5	83.5	82.2	80.6
1986		79.2	78.3										

PRODUCTION-WORKER AVERAGE WEEKLY EARNINGS—IN DOLLARS

1983	354.71	347.77	342.14	351.12	351.39	351.34	356.31	352.91	354.32	360.00	357.29	361.09	370.27
1984	364.11	358.20	353.23	355.32	358.80	363.10	365.72	361.78	365.71	373.18	370.06	366.92	377.17
1985	374.40	370.54	368.54	355.73	375.34	373.46	374.26	373.18	376.67	377.60	374.40	373.07	383.25
1986		378.40	376.66										

PRODUCTION-WORKER AVERAGE HOURLY EARNINGS—IN DOLLARS

1983	8.98	8.94	8.98	8.98	9.01	9.01	8.93	8.98	8.97	9.00	8.91	8.96	9.12
1984	9.08	9.00	8.92	8.95	8.97	9.01	9.03	9.09	9.12	9.26	9.16	9.15	9.29
1985	9.36	9.31	9.33	9.32	9.36	9.29	9.31	9.40	9.37	9.44	9.36	9.35	9.51
1986		9.46	9.44										

PRODUCTION-WORKER AVERAGE WEEKLY HOURS

1983	39.5	38.9	38.1	39.1	39.0	39.3	39.9	39.3	39.5	40.0	40.1	40.3	40.6
1984	40.1	39.8	39.6	39.7	40.0	40.3	40.5	39.8	40.1	40.3	40.4	40.1	40.6
1985	40.0	39.8	39.5	39.9	40.1	40.2	40.2	39.7	40.2	40.0	40.0	39.9	40.3
1986		40.0	39.9										

PRODUCTION-WORKER AVERAGE WEEKLY OVERTIME HOURS

1983	2.5	1.7	1.5	2.1	2.1	2.3	2.5	2.5	2.7	3.0	3.3	3.1	3.3
1984	3.1	3.0	3.0	2.9	2.9	3.0	3.2	3.1	3.4	3.3	3.3	3.1	3.1
1985	2.7	2.5	2.6	2.6	2.6	2.7	2.9	3.0	2.9	2.9	2.8	2.6	2.8
1986		2.7	2.5										

SIC 3446—ARCHITECTURAL METAL WORK

ALL EMPLOYEES—IN THOUSANDS

1983	27.0	26.9	26.5	26.0	26.3	26.6	27.3	26.7	27.1	27.5	27.6	28.0	28.0
1984	27.8	27.4	27.2	27.1	27.3	27.7	28.2	28.2	28.0	28.3	28.3	28.0	27.8
1985	28.3	28.1	28.2	28.3	28.5	28.3	29.1	28.7	27.8	28.2	28.3	28.0	27.8
1986		27.9	27.8										

PRODUCTION WORKERS—IN THOUSANDS

1983	18.7	18.6	18.3	17.8	18.0	18.3	18.9	18.3	18.8	19.0	19.0	19.3	19.7
1984	19.8	19.5	19.2	19.3	19.4	20.0	20.2	20.2	20.1	20.2	20.1	20.0	19.8
1985	20.3	19.7	19.9	20.0	20.3	20.3	21.0	20.8	19.9	20.3	20.5	20.3	20.2
1986		20.2	20.2										

See footnotes at end of tables.

SIC 3446—ARCHITECTURAL METAL WORK (Con.)

PRODUCTION-WORKER AVERAGE WEEKLY EARNINGS—IN DOLLARS

Year	Ann. Avg.	Jan.	Feb.	Mar.	Apr.	May	June	July	Aug.	Sept.	Oct.	Nov.	Dec.
1983	358.97	350.27	337.08	350.24	359.07	357.06	358.83	347.73	365.33	370.60	377.94	371.60	363.80
1984	365.08	355.37	364.72	363.41	372.19	364.41	377.52	368.05	358.75	357.94	357.78	363.20	374.82
1985	341.82	362.70	347.49	356.00	345.54	347.53	337.11	323.98	330.37	328.16	330.57	335.91	358.56
1986		343.26	335.55										

PRODUCTION-WORKER AVERAGE HOURLY EARNINGS—IN DOLLARS

1983	8.82	8.67	8.71	8.80	8.91	8.86	8.86	8.65	8.74	8.93	9.02	8.89	8.83
1984	8.97	8.84	9.05	9.04	9.10	9.02	9.01	8.88	8.88	8.86	8.90	8.99	9.01
1985	8.61	9.00	8.91	8.99	8.86	8.71	8.47	8.35	8.28	8.35	8.39	8.44	8.64
1986		8.56	8.56										

PRODUCTION-WORKER AVERAGE WEEKLY HOURS

1983	40.7	40.4	38.7	39.8	40.3	40.3	40.5	40.2	41.8	41.5	41.9	41.8	41.2
1984	40.7	40.3	40.3	40.2	40.9	40.4	41.9	41.4	40.4	40.4	40.2	40.4	41.6
1985	39.7	40.3	39.0	39.6	39.0	39.9	39.8	38.8	39.9	39.3	39.4	39.8	41.5
1986		40.1	39.2										

PRODUCTION-WORKER AVERAGE WEEKLY OVERTIME HOURS

1983	2.3	2.8	1.7	1.8	2.0	2.3	2.9	1.5	2.7	2.7	2.8	2.3	2.5
1984	2.7	2.3	2.7	2.7	3.0	2.2	3.2	2.8	2.7	2.7	2.5	2.6	2.8
1985	2.9	3.2	1.7	1.9	2.2	2.4	2.6	3.1	3.5	3.1	3.6	4.1	4.1
1986		3.6	3.2										

SIC 345—SCREW MACHINE PRODUCTS, BOLTS, ETC.

ALL EMPLOYEES—IN THOUSANDS

1983	85.4	81.9	82.1	82.5	83.6	84.6	85.7	83.7	85.0	87.0	88.7	90.2	91.2
1984	96.4	92.4	93.6	94.6	95.6	96.3	97.4	95.3	96.8	97.9	98.8	98.8	99.0
1985	97.4	98.9	99.3	99.2	98.8	98.5	97.9	95.3	96.6	96.8	96.2	96.0	95.9
1986		96.0	97.0										

WOMEN EMPLOYEES—IN THOUSANDS

1983	19.4	18.1	18.3	18.5	18.8	19.1	19.3	18.9	19.5	19.9	20.5	20.7	20.9
1984	22.2	21.0	21.4	21.8	22.1	22.4	22.4	21.5	22.2	22.5	22.6	22.6	22.8
1985	22.2	22.8	22.8	22.7	22.4	22.4	22.4	21.5	21.9	21.9	21.9	21.9	21.9
1986		21.7	21.9										

PRODUCTION WORKERS—IN THOUSANDS

1983	63.6	60.3	60.5	61.0	61.9	62.6	63.5	61.8	63.3	65.0	66.7	67.9	68.9
1984	73.6	70.0	71.3	72.0	72.9	73.5	74.3	72.6	73.8	75.3	75.9	75.8	75.9
1985	74.5	75.7	76.2	76.2	75.7	75.6	75.0	72.6	73.8	74.0	73.5	73.0	73.1
1986		73.1	73.9										

PRODUCTION-WORKER AVERAGE WEEKLY EARNINGS—IN DOLLARS

1983	348.47	322.37	319.49	331.45	336.40	340.94	344.73	347.62	349.73	360.76	365.05	371.92	380.59
1984	378.81	376.66	379.73	378.42	378.43	376.68	372.77	370.09	375.28	383.96	381.31	380.84	387.97
1985	385.35	383.45	385.10	386.01	382.82	379.32	384.99	375.91	379.89	385.90	387.82	391.78	408.63
1986		396.68	400.18										

PRODUCTION-WORKER AVERAGE HOURLY EARNINGS—IN DOLLARS

1983	8.52	8.33	8.32	8.37	8.41	8.46	8.47	8.52	8.53	8.61	8.63	8.71	8.81
1984	8.83	8.78	8.79	8.78	8.76	8.76	8.73	8.77	8.83	8.95	8.93	8.94	8.96
1985	9.11	8.98	9.04	9.04	9.05	9.01	9.08	9.08	9.11	9.21	9.19	9.24	9.37
1986		9.29	9.35										

-97-
Fitzgerald Case File

U.S. DEPARTMENT OF LABOR, HANDBOOK OF LABOR STATISTICS, 1978

TABLE 113. Employee Compensation, Private Nonagricultural Economy, 1966–76—Continued   EXHIBIT E

Compensation practice	All industries			Manufacturing			Nonmanufacturing		
	Percent of compensation	Dollars per hour		Percent of compensation	Dollars per hour		Percent of compensation	Dollars per hour	
		All hours	Work hours		All hours	Work hours		All hours	Work hours
Office workers, 1976⁶									
Total compensation	100.0	$8.54	$9.43	100.0	$9.61	$10.74	100.0	$8.14	$8.94
Pay for working time	75.7	$6.47	$7.14	73.2	$704	7.86	76.8	$6.25	$6.87
Straight-time pay	74.9	6.40	7.06	72.2	6.94	7.76	76.1	6.20	6.80
Premium pay	.8	.07	.07	1.0	.10	.11	.7	.06	.06
Overtime, weekend, and holiday work	.6	.05	.06	.9	.08	.09	.5	.04	.05
Shift differentials	.1	.01	.01	.1	.01	.02	.1	.01	.01
Pay for leave time (except sick leave)	6.7	.57	.63	7.5	.72	.80	6.3	.51	.56
Vacations	3.9	.33	.36	4.2	.40	.45	3.7	.30	.33
Holidays	2.5	.22	.24	2.9	.28	.31	2.4	.19	.21
Civic and personal leave	.2	.02	.02	.2	.02	.03	.2	.02	.02
Employment payments to vacation and holiday funds	(1)	(1)	(1)	.1	.01	.02	(1)	(1)	(1)
Employer expenditures for retirement programs	9.1	.77	.85	9.2	.89	.99	9.0	.73	.80
Social security	4.0	.34	.37	3.7	.36	.40	4.1	.33	.36
Private pension plans	5.1	.44	.48	5.5	.53	.59	4.9	.40	.44
Employer expenditures for health benefit programs²	5.2	.44	.49	6.1	.58	.65	4.8	.39	.43
Life, accident, and health insurance	3.6	.31	.34	4.5	.44	.49	3.2	.26	.29
Sick leave	1.2	.10	.11	1.1	.10	.12	1.2	.10	.11
Worker's compensation	.4	.04	.04	.5	.04	.05	.4	.03	.04
Employer expenditures for unemployment benefit programs	1.0	.08	.09	1.1	.10	.12	.9	.08	.08
Unemployment insurance	.8	.07	.08	.9	.08	.09	.8	.07	.07
Severance pay	.1	.01	.01	.2	.02	.02	.1	.01	.01
Severance pay funds and supplemental unemployment benefit funds	(1)	(1)	(1)	(1)	(1)	(1)	(1)	(1)	(1)
Nonproduction bonuses	2.0	.17	.19	2.3	.22	.25	1.9	.15	.17
Savings and thrift plans	.4	.03	.04	.6	.06	.07	.3	.02	.02
Wages and salaries (gross payroll)³	85.6	7.31	8.07	84.1	8.08	9.03	86.3	7.02	7.71
Supplements to wages and salaries⁴	14.4	1.23	1.36	15.9	1.53	1.71	13.7	1.12	1.23
Nonoffice workers, 1976⁶									
Total compensation	100.0	$6.08	$6.54	100.0	$6.38	$6.98	100.0	$5.84	$6.20
Pay for working time	77.4	$4.71	$5.06	75.2	$4.80	$5.25	79.4	$4.63	$4.92
Straight-time pay	74.6	4.54	4.88	71.7	4.57	5.00	77.2	4.51	4.79
Premium pay	2.8	.17	.18	3.5	.22	.24	2.2	.13	.14
Overtime weekend, and holiday work	2.4	.15	.16	2.9	.19	.20	2.0	.11	.12
Shift differentials	.4	.02	.03	.6	.04	.04	.2	.01	.01
Pay for leave time (except sick leave)	5.7	.35	.38	6.8	.43	.47	4.8	.28	.30
Vacations	3.1	.19	.21	3.8	.24	.27	2.6	.15	.16
Holidays	2.1	.13	.14	2.6	.17	.16	1.7	.10	.10
Civic and personal leave	0.1	.01	.01	.2	.01	.01	.1	.01	.01
Employer payments to vacation and holiday funds	0.3	.02	.02	.1	.01	.01	.5	.03	.03
Employer expenditures for retirement programs	8.3	.50	.54	8.5	.54	.60	8.0	.47	.50
Social security	4.6	.28	.30	4.5	.28	.31	4.7	.27	.29
Private pension plans	3.7	.22	.24	4.1	.26	.28	3.3	.20	.21
Employer expenditures for health benefit programs²	6.6	.40	.43	7.4	.47	.51	5.9	.34	.37
Life, accident, and health insurance	4.4	.27	.29	5.3	.34	.37	3.6	.21	.22
Sick leave	.6	.04	.04	.6	.04	.04	.7	.04	.04
Worker's compensation	1.5	.09	.10	1.5	.09	.10	1.6	.09	.10
Employer expenditures for unemployment benefit programs	1.5	.09	.10	1.6	.10	.11	1.4	.08	.08
Unemployment insurance	1.3	.08	.08	1.3	.08	.09	1.3	.07	.08
Severance pay	.1	.01	.01	.2	.01	.01	(1)	(1)	(1)
Severance pay funds and supplemental unemployment benefit funds	.1	(1)	(1)	.1	(1)	(1)	.1	(1)	.01
Nonproduction bonuses	.4	.03	.03	.5	.03	.03	.4	.02	.02
Savings and thrift plans	.1	(1)	(1)	.1	(1)	(1)	.1	(1)	(1)
Wages and salaries (gross payroll)³	84.0	5.11	5.49	83.1	5.30	5.80	84.8	4.95	5.26
Supplementals to wages and salaries⁴	16.0	.97	1.05	16.9	1.08	1.18	15.2	.89	.94

¹Less than 0.05 percent, or $0.005.
²Includes other health benefit programs, principally State temporary disability insurance, not presented separately.
³Includes all direct payments to workers. They consist of pay for time worked, pay for vacations, holidays, sick leave, and civic and personal leave; severance pay; and nonproduction bonuses.
⁴Includes all employer expenditures for compensation other than for wages and salaries. They consist of expenditures for retirement programs (including direct pay to pensioners under pay-as-you-go private pension plans); expenditures for health benefit programs (except sick leave); expenditures for unemployment benefit programs (except severance pay); payments to vacation and holiday funds; and payments to savings and thrift plans.
⁵Nonoffice workers in manufacturing are equivalent to production workers.
⁶Relates to establishments employing 20 or more workers.

NOTE: Because of rounding, sums of individual items may not equal totals.

Fitzgerald Case File

EXHIBIT F

New York State College of Human Ecology, Cornell University, *The Dollar Value of Household Work*, 1980

Table 4. Average Annual Dollar Value of Time Contributed by Various Members in All Household Work (All Values to Nearest $100)

Number of Children	Age in Years	Employed-Wife Households			Non-employed-Wife Households		
		Wife	Husband		Wife	Husband	
0	under 25	$ 4,700	$1,800		$ 7,000	$1,100	
	25–39	5,000	1,900		8,000	1,600	
	40–54	5,900	1,100		8,400	2,100	
	55 and over	6,000	1,500		7,400	2,700	
	Youngest Child	Wife	Husband	Teens	Wife	Husband	Teens
1	12–17	$ 6,700	$2,400	$1,400	$ 9,600	$2,700	$1,200
	6–11	8,000	1,500	–	9,400	2,000	–
	2–5	6,200	2,000	–	9,100	2,400	–
	1	8,300	600	–	9,900	2,300	–
	under 1	*	*	–	10,900	2,100	–
2	12–17	6,300	2,100	1,000	10,000	2,200	1,100
	6–11	7,200	2,000	1,100	9,900	2,100	1,100
	2–5	8,300	2,400	1,500	11,000	2,200	900
	1	8,400	5,000	*	11,700	2,200	*
	under 1	10,200	2,100	*	12,600	2,000	*
3	12–17	5,000	2,100	1,100	9,000	1,400	1,000
	6–11	8,600	2,000	1,700	9,900	2,200	1,600
	2–5	10,200	2,800	*	10,700	1,900	1,000
	1	11,500	3,200	*	11,600	2,200	1,400
	under 1	8,700	2,800	*	13,300	2,000	*
4	12–17	8,700	1,900	1,700	8,400	1,400	1,000
	6–11	7,200	1,400	1,100	10,700	1,900	1,100
	2–5	*	*	*	12,000	2,000	1,100
	1	*	*	*	11,800	2,600	800
	under 1	*	*	*	13,700	2,600	*
5–6	12–17	*	*	*	–	–	–
	6–11	*	*	*	11,500	2,800	1,700
	2–5	*	*	*	12,000	2,100	900
	1	*	*	*	9,900	700	*
	under 1	*	*	*	13,600	2,600	1,000
7–9	6–11	–	–	–	*	*	*
	2–5	*	*	*	11,900	2,900	1,400
	1	–	–	–	*	*	*
	under 1	–	–	–	15,200	2,600	*

* Averages not calculated because there were fewer than 4 cases. — No cases.

For husband.
$____per____ (day, week, month or year)
For each teen-ager
$____per____ (day, week, month or year)
Total for whole family
$____per____ (day, week, month or year)

These figures can be meaningful to your family only as you decide whether the contributions of time from various members for the family's work is distributed in the "best way" for your family.

By examining the work-leisure needs of all family members, it may be that new solutions can be found in your family for sharing household work without significant losses in family services. It is important that a family recognize both the costs and benefits that are associated with work for the family and the employment of the husband, wife and older children if work decisions are to be made rationally. What are you willing to give up to gain what you want? What are the costs as well as the benefits of alternative choices? Many of the costs and benefits are intangible and cannot be measured; nevertheless, calculating a dollar equivalent for this set of household services may increase your chances of making satisfactory decisions about the use of each family member's time.

Finding the economic measure of the value of such services need not mean that you will ignore the nondollar values, rewards and satisfactions the family receives from them. True value is decided by the individual and the family; the money value can be one objective

EXHIBIT G

TABLE 122. The Consumer Price Index for Selected Items and Groups Other Than Food, 1947–77—Continued

[1967=100 unless otherwise specified]

Item and group	1960	1961	1962	1963	1964	1965	1966	1968	1969	1970	1971	1972	1973	1974	1975	1976	1977
Housing—Continued																	
Household furnishings and operation—Continued																	
House furnishings—Continued																	
Appliances[5]	117.9	115.2	111.6	109.2	107.4	103.9	100.7	101.2	102.4	104.1	105.5	105.8	105.5	109.7	118.4	123.3	126.0
Appliances, excluding radio and T.V.	112.1	109.8	107.2	105.2	104.0	101.6	99.9	102.1	104.3	106.9	109.1	109.7	109.8	115.6	128.1	135.3	140.1
Washing machines, electric, automatic	110.7	107.4	104.5	103.0	101.6	100.2	99.7	102.5	104.6	107.3	109.4	110.5	111.0	117.1	131.9	141.0	145.5
Vacuum cleaners, canister type	118.1	115.5	109.3	104.8	102.8	101.3	100.8	100.9	102.6	102.6	103.8	103.8	104.1	107.6	116.7	121.0	125.3
Refrigerators or refrigerator-freezer, electric	116.8	115.2	112.5	109.6	107.4	104.2	100.2	101.3	103.1	105.8	108.1	108.1	108.3	114.6	128.7	134.8	139.7
Ranges, free standing, gas or electric	106.6	104.4	104.0	103.2	102.5	101.1	99.2	102.7	105.4	108.5	111.0	110.9	110.3	115.8	130.0	138.7	143.4
Clothes dryers, electric, automatic	----	----	----	----	105.5	103.0	100.0	103.1	105.2	108.4	112.4	114.2	114.4	121.4	136.7	148.6	155.1
Garbage disposal units	----	----	----	----	100.5	99.9	99.9	102.1	105.2	109.1	110.1	111.0	111.9	117.9	128.6	134.3	139.3
Other house furnishings:																	
Dinnerware, earthenware	83.8	84.7	86.8	89.6	91.1	93.0	95.6	102.8	106.6	111.5	117.8	124.1	131.0	148.8	174.6	190.6	203.7
Flatware, stainless steel	----	----	----	----	98.0	96.7	98.3	111.6	116.7	119.1	120.4	124.8	132.0	147.7	173.3	181.3	185.9
Table lamps, with shade	----	----	----	----	93.9	93.6	96.1	103.2	109.5	116.0	121.0	123.8	128.2	135.7	145.5	148.2	152.0
Electric drills, hand held	----	----	----	----	103.9	102.1	100.3	104.2	108.3	107.6	106.7	106.5	106.7	113.4	123.9	128.3	131.0
Housekeeping supplies:																	
Laundry soaps and detergents	97.0	96.0	85.8	96.6	96.3	96.6	98.0	101.1	102.3	106.0	109.8	111.2	113.4	133.6	161.9	174.9	186.0
Paper napkins	84.7	83.5	84.8	88.4	91.3	92.2	95.9	105.4	110.5	118.7	126.7	131.1	138.6	166.8	206.9	219.9	238.7
Toilet tissue	95.3	95.1	94.6	93.9	93.8	94.0	96.3	105.1	109.0	117.8	123.6	124.9	128.4	158.3	208.0	234.4	264.7
Housekeeping services:																	
Domestic service, general	75.4	76.5	78.6	80.2	83.6	87.8	92.4	110.0	117.4	126.8	133.8	139.1	147.3	175.7	196.1	211.2	221.6
housework	----	----	----	----	86.6	89.9	93.9	108.0	115.7	123.0	130.0	136.3	142.8	165.4	191.5	214.6	227.3
Babysitter service	79.2	80.0	80.6	92.9	96.0	96.4	97.2	113.7	117.0	117.7	138.1	146.6	146.6	170.5	175.4	222.3	225.6
Postal charges																	
Laundry, flatwork, finished service	----	----	----	----	83.3	86.7	92.4	106.5	115.5	124.3	133.3	138.7	148.9	170.1	187.3	203.9	222.3
Licensed day care service, preschool child	----	----	----	----	86.5	88.8	94.1	105.5	109.6	114.5	118.2	122.5	130.5	142.1	154.2	162.8	172.2
Washing machine repairs	----	----	----	----	88.8	91.5	95.2	105.7	114.5	123.8	135.3	140.7	148.7	166.4	187.0	200.4	210.4
Apparel and upkeep	89.6	90.4	90.9	91.9	92.7	93.7	96.1	105.4	111.5	116.1	119.8	122.3	126.8	136.2	142.3	147.6	154.2
Apparel commodities	90.3	90.8	91.2	92.0	92.8	93.6	96.0	105.6	111.9	116.5	120.1	122.7	127.1	136.1	141.2	145.8	151.6
Apparel commodities, less footwear	91.5	92.0	92.1	93.0	93.8	94.5	96.2	105.7	111.9	116.3	119.9	122.3	126.5	135.7	140.6	144.9	150.6
Men's and boys'	88.9	89.9	90.4	91.6	92.8	94.0	96.5	105.7	112.4	117.1	120.3	121.9	126.4	136.4	142.2	147.2	154.0
Men's:																	
Topcoats, wool or all-weather coats	83.2	86.4	87.5	89.8	----	----	97.0	107.1	114.1	119.3	122.3	125.8	132.2	141.2	143.2	149.4	154.6
Suits, year round weight	79.8	81.8	82.3	85.0	89.4	92.4	96.4	106.7	116.6	123.9	129.0	130.3	133.1	135.0	139.2	140.8	140.8
Jackets, lightweight	----	----	----	----	91.4	93.3	95.8	104.7	112.6	113.1	112.5	114.2	118.2	125.9	134.4	139.1	146.8
Slacks, wool or wool blends	88.0	89.1	88.0	90.2	91.4	93.4	97.1	105.4	111.4	115.4	116.8	115.7	116.9	118.5	120.1	118.6	118.6
Slacks, cotton or manmade blends	99.0	98.4	97.2	95.3	94.9	95.9	97.7	105.9	115.3	124.5	132.3	137.6	140.3	142.2	143.0	145.9	151.1
Trousers, work, cotton	93.7	93.7	93.5	93.8	94.4	95.0	96.3	103.8	107.8	109.3	113.0	114.8	120.2	139.2	151.0	161.0	174.0
Shirt, work, cotton	87.3	87.2	88.6	90.8	91.7	92.7	94.9	102.3	105.8	109.2	113.3	115.2	120.9	140.7	151.3	159.1	173.2
Shirts, business, polyester/cotton	93.4	95.6	95.7	96.3	96.6	97.0	99.2	104.3	107.5	110.5	112.7	112.6	113.9	123.0	127.7	133.1	143.5
T-shirts, chiefly cotton	89.6	89.9	93.1	95.0	95.0	95.2	95.8	108.4	115.0	118.8	119.0	117.9	122.0	141.4	153.5	159.2	176.6
Socks, cotton or stretch nylon	94.2	94.5	95.2	95.3	94.9	94.6	96.3	107.0	112.3	114.9	115.5	115.8	117.3	122.2	129.1	134.7	139.2
Handkerchiefs, cotton	----	----	----	----	98.0	98.4	99.6	103.4	109.8	113.0	114.9	116.4	120.7	141.4	153.2	161.9	171.6

See footnotes at end of table.

U.S. Dept. of Labor, *Handbook of Labor Statistics*, 1978

EXHIBIT H

TABLE 122. The Consumer Price Index for Selected Items and Groups Other Than Food, 1947-77—Continued

[1967=100 unless otherwise specified]

Item and group	1947	1948	1949	1950	1951	1952	1953	1954	1955	1956	1957	1958	1959
Housing—Continued													
Household furnishings and operation—Continued													
House furnishings—Continued													
Appliances[5]	140.8	147.4	140.9	138.3	146.4	141.2	138.8	132.8	126.4	120.3	120.6	118.6	118.7
Appliances, excluding radio and T.V.	130.5	141.0	137.9	135.1	143.8	141.9	140.4	135.9	129.3	120.1	117.7	113.8	113.6
Washing machines, electric, automatic	112.7	121.2	119.6	118.1	126.2	126.7	124.8	121.8	118.5	115.7	117.1	115.8	113.6
Vacuum cleaners, canister type	149.5	144.7	145.6	144.7	154.4	157.9	163.5	164.2	158.3	141.8	132.4	124.9	120.4
Refrigerators or refrigerator-freezer, electric	174.5	192.7	186.8	182.7	192.4	185.1	178.1	166.0	156.0	134.6	123.8	119.6	119.2
Ranges, free standing, gas or electric	101.7	107.8	103.8	100.6	112.1	110.9	111.3	109.6	107.0	106.4	108.4	107.6	107.3
Clothes dryers, electric, automatic	------	------	------	------	------	------	------	------	------	------	------	------	------
Garbage disposal units	------	------	------	------	------	------	------	------	------	------	------	------	------
Other house furnishings:													
Dinnerware, earthenware	52.8	56.1	59.0	59.3	63.1	65.3	66.4	68.5	69.5	74.0	77.7	80.9	81.4
Flatware, stainless steel	------	------	------	------	------	------	------	------	------	------	------	------	------
Table lamps, with shade	------	------	------	------	------	------	------	------	------	------	------	------	------
Electric drills, hand held	------	------	------	------	------	------	------	------	------	------	------	------	------
Housekeeping supplies:													
Laundry soaps and detergents	95.5	98.1	82.4	77.8	88.7	82.7	82.2	86.1	87.6	89.8	93.9	97.3	97.5
Paper napkins	------	------	------	------	------	------	84.1	83.9	84.4	84.8	86.0	86.9	85.7
Toilet tissue	80.7	91.0	85.0	81.8	90.8	88.9	88.5	88.1	86.8	86.3	89.9	91.8	93.3
Housekeeping services:													
Domestic service, general housework	49.4	50.1	50.3	50.4	52.5	56.4	59.9	60.8	61.2	62.9	65.3	67.2	70.4
Babysitter service	------	------	------	------	------	------	------	------	------	------	------	------	------
Postal charges	48.8	48.8	52.7	53.1	54.2	59.7	60.6	65.2	65.2	65.2	65.4	70.2	76.5
Laundry, flatwork, finished service	------	------	------	------	------	------	------	------	------	------	------	------	------
Licensed day care service, preschool child	------	------	------	------	------	------	------	------	------	------	------	------	------
Washing machine repairs	------	------	------	------	------	------	------	------	------	------	------	------	------
Apparel and upkeep	78.2	83.3	80.1	79.0	86.1	85.3	84.6	84.5	84.1	85.8	87.3	87.5	88.2
Apparel commodities	80.4	85.4	82.0	81.1	88.7	87.7	86.7	86.3	85.8	87.3	88.2	88.2	89.0
Apparel commodities, less footwear	85.9	91.1	86.8	85.2	92.0	91.2	90.3	89.6	88.9	89.8	90.6	90.4	90.5
Men's and boys'	78.3	82.7	80.5	80.1	86.7	87.1	86.4	86.0	85.0	86.4	87.8	87.3	87.2
Men's:													
Topcoats, wool or all-weather coats	67.6	70.5	70.6	71.2	78.7	80.0	78.4	78.9	78.0	79.2	80.1	79.2	80.3
Suits, year round weight	57.4	66.1	65.9	65.4	73.3	72.9	72.0	73.0	73.3	74.3	76.4	77.5	78.0
Jackets, lightweight	------	------	------	------	------	------	------	------	------	------	------	------	------
Slacks, wool or wool blends	77.7	81.2	82.6	80.7	85.9	84.5	82.7	83.5	84.5	85.6	87.2	87.6	87.4
Slacks, cotton or manmade blends	------	------	------	------	------	105.6	104.4	101.4	101.6	101.8	102.8	99.1	
Trousers, work, cotton	87.2	88.8	85.7	86.6	94.6	93.0	91.9	90.0	88.6	91.9	93.3	92.7	91.8
Shirt, work, cotton	85.5	85.9	80.3	80.9	86.9	83.4	80.9	79.2	78.2	83.2	86.0	86.3	85.8
Shirts, business, polyester/cotton	94.1	94.5	85.3	84.0	90.4	88.3	88.7	88.4	87.6	87.1	88.2	88.5	89.3
T-shirts, chiefly cotton	87.8	88.5	81.9	84.5	96.1	87.9	86.5	85.8	85.8	87.3	88.9	88.2	88.2
Socks, cotton or stretch nylon	88.5	86.2	82.8	83.9	91.3	90.7	89.3	91.0	91.0	93.5	94.2	93.3	93.5
Handkerchiefs, cotton	------	------	------	------	------	------	------	------	------	------	------	------	------

See footnotes at end of table.

U.S. Dept. of Labor, <u>Handbook of Labor Statistics</u>, 1978

EXHIBIT I

U.S. Dept. of Labor, Bulletin 1570-2

Table 1. Revised Equivalence Scale[1] For Urban Families of Different Size, Age, and Composition

[4-person family-husband, age 35 to 54, wife, 2 children, older 6 to 15 = 100]

Size and type of family[2]	Age of head			
	Under 35	35-54	55-64	65 or over
One person	35	36	32	28
Two persons: average[3]	47	59	59	52
Husband and wife	49	60	59	51
One parent and child	40	57	60	58
Three persons: average[3]	62	81	86	77
Husband, wife, child under 6	62	69	--	--
Husband, wife, child 6-15	62	82	88	81
Husband, wife, child 16-17	--	91	88	--
Husband, wife, child 18 or over	--	82	85	77
One parent, 2 children	67	76	82	75
Four persons: average[3]	74	99	109	91
Husband, wife, 2 children, (older under 6)	72	80	--	--
Husband, wife, 2 children, (older 6-15)	77	100	105	95
Husband, wife, 2 children, (older 16-17)	--	113	125	--
Husband, wife, 2 children, (older 18 or over)	--	96	110	89
One parent, 3 children	88	96	--	--
Five persons: average[3]	94	118	124	--
Husband, wife, 3 children, (oldest under 6)	87	97	--	--
Husband, wife, 3 children, (oldest 6-15)	96	116	120	--
Husband, wife, 3 children, (oldest 16-17)	--	128	138	--
Husband, wife, 3 children, (oldest 18 or over)	--	119	124	--
One parent, 4 children	108	117	--	--
Six persons or more: average[3]	111	138	143	--
Husband, wife, 4 children or more, (oldest under 6)	101	--	--	--
Husband, wife, 4 children or more, (oldest 6-15)	110	132	140	--
Husband, wife, 4 children or more, (oldest 16-17)	--	146	--	--
Husband, wife, 4 children or more, (oldest 18 or over)	--	149	--	--
One parent, 5 children or more	125	137	--	--

[1] The scale values shown here are the percentages of the cost of goods and services for family consumption of the base family (4 persons--husband, age 35-54, wife, 2 children, older child 6-15 years) required to provide the same level of living for urban families of different size, age, and composition.

[2] Husband-wife and one-parent families with their own children (including adopted and stepchildren) present, but with no other persons living with the family.

[3] Scale values for individual family types weighted by the number of families of each type in the universe. The averages include some types for which values were not shown separately because of the small number of such families in the sample.

[4] Revised.

SOURCE: Derived from BLS Survey of Consumer Expenditures, 1960-61.

Fitzgerald Case File

HARVEY GELBER, Ph.D.
Professor of Economics
University of Nita
Nita City, Nita

June 10, YR-1

Thomas Busch, Esq.
2000 Johnson Drive
Wellington, Nita

Dear Mr. Busch:

Enclosed please find my Economic Analysis Report concerning the death of Johnny Fitzgerald. Also enclosed is a copy of my resume for your files.

Please treat this letter as a statement for my services. Since I have spent ten hours on this matter, my fee will be $2000.00. Should you find it necessary for my appearance at a deposition or trial, my rate for those appearances will be $100.00 per hour.

Thank you for the opportunity to consult on this matter.

Sincerely,

Harvey Gelber, Ph.D.

RESUME

HARVEY GELBER

Present Position: Professor of Economics
University of Nita
Nita City, Nita

Education: B.S., Economics
University of Kansas, YR-18

Ph.D., Economics
University of Nita, YR-14

Teaching: Taught economics at the undergraduate and graduate level at the University of Nita for fourteen years. Taught at numerous seminars in industry and delivered numerous papers at conferences and seminars.

Research: Directed graduate research.
Research and publication in economic journals on the loss to survivors of death of a family member.

Grants: National Science Foundation
Social Science Research Council
Center for Comparative Studies, University of Nita
Nita Law Enforcement Commission

ON—TRACK EQUIPMENT ACCIDENT/INCIDENT REPORT
—IMMEDIATE NOTIFICATION—

WIRE REPORT F-27
CONDUCTOR AND/OR MAINTENANCE MACHINE OPERATORS

ALL "FAILED JOURNALS" AND "BROKEN WHEELS" OCCURRING ON MAIN OR BRANCH TRACKS MUST BE REPORTED.

Complete all appropriate sections of this report and send to Superintendent and to Region Vice President by quickest means of communication)

To: **Supt.** Date: **10/26/YR-2** From: **P. Rombach** Division: **Investigation**

Types or types of on-track equipment involvement (Check all appropriate boxes)

- ☐ Derailment - — Complete pages 1 and 2
- ☐ Collision between on-track equipment consists — Complete pages 1, 2, and 3
- ☒ Rail-highway grade crossing collision — Complete pages 1, 2, and 4
- ☐ Obstruction incident — Complete pages 1 and 2
- ☐ Fire damage to locomotives, cars or contents — Complete pages 1, 2, and 5
- ☐ Hazardous material incident — Complete pages 1 and 2
  Form 15957 for each car of hazardous material derailed or damaged
- ☐ Casualty to person(s) — Complete pages 1 and 2
  Form 15016 for each casualty

(Hot boxes, broken knuckles, sticking brakes, etc., which do not result in any of the above, and require repairs only to that part involved, need not be reported on F-27 On-Track Equipment Accident/Incident Report.)

F-27 INIT	F-27 NUMBER	ACCIDENT DATE YEAR MONTH DAY	TIME HOUR MIN	SUB-DIVN	STATE CODE	MAIN TRACK BLOCKED? (Y or N) **Y**
		YR-2 10 20	17 47		NT	CLEARED BY TIME **1900** DATE **10/20/YR-2**

ROAD LINE SGMT.	MILEPOST LOCATION (100ths)	TRACK OWNER	NEAREST STATION NO	NAME OF NEAREST STATION
	.	N&W	047	WELLINGTON

TYPE OF INCIDENT: 12
- 01 DERAILMENT
- 02 HEAD-ON COLLISION
- 03 READ—END COLLISION
- 04 SIDE COLLISION
- 05 RAKING COLLISION
- 06 BROKEN TRAIN COLL
- 07 HGX COLLISION
- 08 RR CROSSING COLL
- 09 OBSTRUCTION INCIDENT
- 10 EXPLOSION-DENOTATION
- 11 FIRE-VIOLENT RUPTURE
- 12 OTHER **R-H**

TEMP. (Degrees): 58
VISIBILITY: 2 (1—DAWN 2—DAY 3—DUSK 4—DARK)
WEATHER: 1 (1—CLEAR 2—CLOUDY 3—RAIN 4—FOG 5—SLEET 6—SNOW)

METHOD(S) OF OPERATION = PRIMARY **B** - SECONDARY - ADDITIONAL
- A—NON-ABS
- B—INTERLOCKING
- C—CAB SIGNAL
- D—ABS
- E—CTC
- F—AUTO. TRAIN STOP
- G—YARD RULES
- H—TIMETABLE
- I—RADIO
- K—VERBAL PERMISSION
- L—TRAIN ORDERS (INCL. TWC)
- M—OTHER
- N—YARD LIMITS (ON MAIN TRACK WITHIN YARD LIMITS)

ACCIDENT AT TURNOUT?	ACCIDENT IN CURVE	TRACK NAME OR NUMBER	TYPE OF TRACK
2 (1-YES 2-NO)	2 (1-YES 2-NO)	SINGLE MAIN	1 (1-MAIN 2-YARD 3-SIDING 4-INDUSTRY)

FRA TRACK CLASS	COUNTY OR PROVIDENCE IN WHICH ACCIDENT OCCURED
4 (X-EXCEPTED, 1-CLASS 1, 2-CLASS 2, 3-CLASS 3, 4-CLASS 4, 5-CLASS 5, 6-CLASS 6)	DOUGLAS

PRIMARY CAUSE	CONTRIB. CAUSE	LOCOMOTIVE CAUSED? L-YES	BROKEN RAIL WT.	YEAR RAIL LAID	EXAMPLE: EXPRESS 1958 AS 958

SYSTEM OR FOREIGN RESPONSIBILITY	TERMINAL? ENTER "T" IF:	REPORTABLE TO FRA?	FOREIGN CARRIER ACCIDENT REPORT NUMBER
S (S-SYSTEM F-FOREIGN)	DENVER, KANSAS CITY, OR, TWIN CITIES	R-REP	

NAME OF INDUSTRY IF TRACK OWNER IS "XX" (INDUSTRY)

DESCRIPTION OF ACCIDENT:
Auto ran into freight train XT471 (4 engines, 85 cars) at cars 1/2 Crossing # 74647C, County Road, Wellington

CASUALTIES TO PERSONS—LIST AND COMPLETE FORM 15016 FOR EACH CASUALTY INVOLVED

FI	MI	LAST NAME	STREET ADDRESS	CITY OR TOWN	STATE
J		Fitzgerald	16 Meadowbrook Lane	Wellington	NT

SIGNATURE: _____ TITLE: **Investigator** DATE: **10/26/YR-2**
FORM 15012 9-84 Printed In U.S.A.

Fitzgerald Case File

PAGE 2: INFORMATION FOR CONSIST NO. 1 INVOLVED IN ACCIDENT

CONSIST OWNER	TYPE OF EQUIPMENT				
N&W	A	A—FREIGHT TRAIN B—PSGR. TRAIN C—MIXED TRAIN	E—SINGLE CAR F—MOTOR CAR G—HI-RAIL CAR	H—PUSH CAR I—ON TRACK MAINT. MACHINE J—CUT OF CARS	K—SWITCH ENGINE L—SW. ENG. WITH CARS M—LITE UNITS

SPEED OF CONSIST	SPEED EST. OR RECORDED		POSITION OF CONSIST		
48	E	E-EST. R-REC.	1	1-TRAIN (UNITS PULLING) 2-TRAIN (UNITS PUSHING) 3-TRAIN (STANDING)	4-CAR(S) (MOVING) 5-CAR(S) STANDING 6-LIGHT LOCOS (MOVING)	7-LIGHT LOCOS (STANDING) 8-OTHER

TIMETABLE DIRECTION		HEADLIGHT		(HGX ONLY)	AMBER/STROBE		(HGX ONLY)	REFLECTORIZED (HGX ONLY)	MARKINGS =
1	1-NORTH 3-EAST 2-SOUTH 4-WEST	1	1-ON 2-OFF 3-N/A		3	1-ON 2-OFF	3-NOT EQUIPPED	1	1-YES 2-NO 3-UNKNOWN

WHISTLE SOUNDED?		BELL RINGING?		CONSIST IDENTIFICATION NUMBER
1	1-YES 2-NO 3-NOT EQUIPPED	1	1-YES 2-NO 3-NOT EQUIPPED	1563

TOTAL EQUIPMENT DAMAGE E/A THIS CONSIST	TOTAL 'FRA' TRACK DAMAGE E/A THIS CONSIST	DAMAGE TO LOCOMOTIVES ON E/A THIS CONSIST

DAMAGE TO CARS ON E/A THIS CONSIST	DAMAGE TO NON-RAILROAD E/A PROPERTY	DAMAGE TO BRIDGES E/A

DAMAGE TO SIGNALS DUE TO E/A THIS CONSIST	DAMAGE TO COMMUNICATIONS E/A DUE TO THIS CONSIST	DAMAGE TO RAILROAD E/A STRUCTURES

NUMBER FATALITIES ON THIS CONSIST	NUMBER INJURED ON THIS CONSIST (REP FRA)	WAS THIS CONSIST UNATTENDED AT TIME OF THE ACCIDENT?
0	0	2 (1-YES 2-NO)

INFORMATION FOR HAZARDOUS MATERIAL CARS IN THIS CONSIST	NO. CARS CARRYING	NO. CARS DAMAGED ON DERAILED	NO. CARS RELEASING HAZARDOUS MATERIAL	NUMBER OF PERSONS EVACUATED

FIRST CAR OR LOCOMOTIVE OF THIS CONSIST INVOLVED IN THE ACCIDENT	INITIAL	NUMBER	POSITION	LOADED OR EMPTY? L—LOAD E—EMPTY

CAR OR LOCOMOTIVE UNIT IN THIS CONSIST CAUSING THE ACCIDENT (MECHANICAL ONLY)	INITIAL	NUMBER	POSITION	LOADED OR EMPTY? L—LOAD E—EMPTY

NUMBER OF LOCOMOTIVE UNITS IN THIS CONSIST	HEAD END	MID—MANUAL	MID—REMOTE	REAR-END MANUAL	REAR-END REMOTE
	4				

NUMBER OF LOCOMOTIVE UNITS IN THIS CONSIST DERAILED	HEAD END	MID—MANUAL	MID—REMOTE	REAR-END MANUAL	REAR-END REMOTE

NOTE: IF OWNERSHIP OF LOCOMOTIVE UNITS IS OTHER THAN BN, INDICATE OWNER-

LOCOMOTIVE IDENTIFICATION NO.s IN THIS CONSIST (FROM HEAD-END, 1st THRU 6TH:	NUMBER	NUMBER	NUMBER	NUMBER	NUMBER	NUMBER
LOCOMOTIVE IDENTIFICATION NUMBERS IN THIS CONSIST (7th Through 12th If Appropriate):	NUMBER	NUMBER	NUMBER	NUMBER	NUMBER	NUMBER

NUMBER OF CARS IN THIS CONSIST	LOADED FREIGHT	PSGR LOADED	EMPTY FREIGHT	PSGR EMPTY	CAB	NUMBER OF CARS DERAILED IN CONSIST	LOADED FREIGHT	PSGR LOADED	EMPTY FREIGHT	PSGR EMPTY	CAB
	21		64				1				

RAILROAD ACCOUNT CARS IN:	TYPE OF SERVICE (FRT TRAINS, CUTS OF CARS, LOCO CONSISTS)				
	R	C-UNIT COAL G-UNIT GRAIN O-UNIT ORE	R-REGULAR FREIGHT T-UNIT TACONITE		

TRAILING TONS	NUMBER OF CREW MEMBERS ON THIS CONSIST	ENGINEERS	FIREPERSONS	CONDUCTORS	BRAKEPERSONS
4033		1	1	1	1

ENGINEER— ON DUTY	HRS	MIN	NAME OF ENGINEER ON THIS CONSIST	FI	MI	LAST NAME
	4	20		S		SMOLEN

CONDUCTOR— ON DUTY	HRS	MIN	NAME OF CONDUCTOR ON THIS CONSIST	FI	MI	LAST NAME
	4	20		R		APRIL

PAGE 4: COMPLETE THIS PAGE FOR ALL RAIL-HIGHWAY GRADE CROSSING ACCIDENTS

Field	Value	Options
OCCURANCE CODE	6 0 5	601—PEDESTRIAN STRUCK BY TRAIN / 602—MOTOR VEHICLE STRUCK BY TRAIN / 603—OTHER VEHICLE, MACHINE, OR ANIMAL STRUCK BY TRAIN / 604-PEDESTRIAN RAN INTO TRAIN OR PASSED OVER-THRU-UNDER CARS / 605-MOTOR VEHICLE RAN INTO TRAIN / 609-OTHER ACCIDENT AT RAIL-HWY GRADE CROSSING SITE
TYPE OF HIGHWAY USER	A	A-AUTO B-TRUCK C-TRUCK-TRAILER D-BUS E-SCHOOL BUS F-MOTORCYCLE G-PEDESTRIAN H-BICYCLE I-FARM VEHICLE J-GASOLINE TRANSPORT K-OTHER
DIRECTION OF HIGHWAY USER	3	1-NORTH 2-SOUTH 3-EAST 4-WEST
SPEED OF HWY USER	50 Est.	
POSITION OF HIGHWAY USER	3	1-STALLED ON CROSSING 2-STOPPED ON CROSSING 3-MOVING OVER CROSSING
MOTORIST ACTION	3	1-DROVE AROUND OR THRU GATES 2-STOPPED AND THEN PROCEEDED 3-DID NOT STOP 4-OTHER 5-UNKNOWN
SECOND TRAIN INVOLVED? (MOTORIST STRUCK BY SECOND TRAIN AT XING)	2	1-YES 2-NO 3-UNKNOWN
MOTORIST PASSED STANDING VEHICLE?	2	1-YES 2-NO 3-UNKNOWN
DRIVER IN VEHICLE?	1	1-YES 2-NO (BLANK IF UNKNOWN)
DRIVER CONDITION	1	1-FATALLY INJURED 2-INJURED (REP-FRA) 3-UNINJURED (NON-REP) (BLANK IF UNKNOWN)
NO. OCCUPANTS FATAL (INCLUDING DRIVER)	1	
NO. OCCUPANTS INJURED (REP FRA) (INCLUDING DRIVER)		
TOTAL NUMBER OF OCCUPANTS (INCLUDE DRIVER)	1	
EST. DAMAGE TO HIGHWAY USER	2000	
HAZARDOUS MATERIALS	4	1-HWY USER TRANSPORTING 2-RAIL CONSIST TRANSPORTING 3-BOTH TRANSPORTING 4-NEITHER TRANSPORTING
DOT-AAR IDENTIFICATION NO.		
ROAD CONDITION	1	1-DRY 2-WET 3-ICY 4-SNOW PACKED
ROAD SURFACE TYPE	3	1-ASPHALT 2-CONCRETE 3-GRAVEL 4-DIRT
HIGHEST LEVEL OF CROSSING PROTECTION	07	01-GATES 02-CANTILEVER FLSHG LIGHTS 03-STANDARD FLSHG LIGHTS 04-WIG WAGS 05-HIGHWAY TRAFFIC SIGNALS 06-AUDIBLE WARNING 07-CROSSBUCKS ONLY 08-STOP SIGNS 09-WATCHMAN 10-FLAGGED BY CREW 11-OTHER 12-NONE
LOCATION OF PROTECTION	3	1-BOTH SIDES OF CROSSING 2-SIDE OF VEHICLE APPROACH 3-OPPOSITE SIDE OF VEHICLE APPROACH (BLANK IF NONE)
HWY TRAFFIC SIGNALS INTERCONNECTED?	2	1-CONNECTED WITHIN 500 FEET 2-NOT CONNECTED WITHIN 500 FT 3-NOT KNOWN
PROTECTION OPERATING?	1	1-YES 2-NO (BLANK)
VIEW RESTRICTED?	4	1-PERMANENT STRUCTURE 2-STANDING RR EQUIPMENT 3-PASSING TRAIN 4-TOPOGRAPHY 5-VEGETATION 6-HIGHWAY VEHICLE 7-OTHER 8-NOT OBSTRUCTED
CROSSING ILLUMINATED?	2	1-YES 2-NO
CROSSING NAME OR NUMBER	74647C COUNTY ROAD	
TYPE OF CROSSING?	C	A-PRIVATE B-CITY C-COUNTY D-STATE E-U.S.
ADVANCE WARNING?		1-YES 2-NO
REPORTABLE BY BN TO FRA?		R-REP. N-NON-REP
REP RAIL ACCT ALSO?		1-YES 2-NO
YEAR OF VEH	YR-7	
MAKE OF VEHICLE	FORD	
MODEL OF VEHICLE	SEDAN 2DR	
OWNER OF VEHICLE	FI: J LAST NAME: FITZGERALD STREET ADDRESS: 16 MEADOWBR CITY: WELLINGTN STATE: NT	
DISPOSITION OF VEHICLE & EST. DAMAGE	Transported by wrecker Totaled	

NAME OF DRIVER OR PEDESTRIAN	FI	MI	LAST NAME	STREET ADDRESS	CITY	STATE
	J		Fitzgerald	16 Meadowbrook Lane	Wellington	NT

☐ INJURED ☐ FATAL ☐ NOT INJURED (X)

NAME OF OCCUPANT	FI	MI	LAST NAME	STREET ADDRESS	CITY	STATE

☐ INJURED ☐ FATAL ☐ NOT INJURED (X)

NAME OF OCCUPANT	FI	MI	LAST NAME	STREET ADDRESS	CITY	STATE

☐ INJURED ☐ FATAL ☐ NOT INJURED (X)

DISPOSITION OF INJURED OR FATAL OCCUPANTS
Removed by Erickson's Mortuary

Fitzgerald Case File

PRINTED IN U.S.A.
FORM CT 25A

NITA AND WESTERN RAILWAY COMPANY
STATEMENT OF TRAIN AND ENGINE CREWS

This form is to be used by all members of train and engine crews in rendering statements concerning accidents in which trains or engines are involved with vehicles or outsiders. The statement must be completed by all crew members and promptly mailed or delivered to Division Superintendent.

Place of accident **WELLINGTON** Division **MAIN**
Date of accident **10-20**, 19 **YR-2** Time **5:47 pm**
Train No. **XT 471** Speed of train **45-50** Direction **NORTH** Weather **CLEAR**
Was horn sounded? **YES** Bell ringing? **YES**
Was stationary headlight burning? **YES** Bright **✓** Dim _____
Was oscillating headlight operating? _____ Bright _____ Dim _____
Damage to Railway equipment **BOX CAR: TRUCKS + SIDE TRACKS OPERABLE**

Make of vehicle **YR-7 FORD** Year **YR-7** License No. **NT D6F-459**
Direction of vehicle **EAST** Speed **50** MPH
Driver **JOHNNY FITZGERALD** Age **25** Address **16 MEADOWBROOK LANE WELLINGTON**
Owner **SAME** Address _____
Other occupants, ages, addresses **NONE**

Damage to vehicle **TOTAL**
Were there any injuries? Yes **✓** No _____

Type of crossing protection **CROSSBUCKS** Operating? Yes _____ No _____
Condition of crossing **GOOD**

Where were you at time of accident? **FIRST ENGINE**
Describe accident (include type and place of brake application, when vehicle, trespasser, pedestrian, or injured person first seen, etc.) **CAR HIT BOXCAR TRAIN INTO EMERGENCY**

Names and addresses of outside witnesses _____

Did police investigate accident? Yes **✓** No _____ (check) State _____ County _____ City _____

Signature **Steve Smolen**
Address **444 CLEARMEADOW DR NITA CITY NT**
Date **10-20**, 19 **YR-2** Occupation **ENGINEER** Age **39**

-117-
Fitzgerald Case File

FORM CT 25A

NITA AND WESTERN RAILWAY COMPANY
STATEMENT OF TRAIN AND ENGINE CREWS

This form is to be used by all members of train and engine crews in rendering statements concerning accidents in which trains or engines are involved with vehicles or outsiders. The statement must be completed by all crew members and promptly mailed or delivered to Division Superintendent.

Place of accident: Wellington Division: Main
Date of accident: Oct 20, 19 YR-2 Time: 5:47 PM
Train No. XT471 Speed of train: 48 Direction: N Weather: Clear
Was horn sounded? Yes Bell ringing? Yes
Was stationary headlight burning? Yes Bright: Yes Dim: ___
Was oscillating headlight operating? ✓ Bright: ___ Dim: ___
Damage to Railway equipment: Box car and tracks — operable

Make of vehicle: Ford Year: YR-7 License No. ___
Direction of vehicle: East Speed: 50 MPH
Driver: ___ Age: ___ Address: ___
Owner: ___ Address: ___
Other occupants, ages, addresses: ___

Damage to vehicle: Wiped Out
Were there any injuries? Yes ✗ No ___

Type of crossing protection: Crossbucks Operating? Yes ✓ No ___
Condition of crossing: Good

Where were you at time of accident? Engine #2
Describe accident (include type and place of brake application, when vehicle, trespasser, pedestrian, or injured person first seen, etc.): Didn't see it — Engine went into Emergency — driver dead at scene —

Names and addresses of outside witnesses: Neighbor — I didn't get his Name — he spoke to the troopers —

Did police investigate accident? Yes ✓ No ___ (check) State ___ County ___ City ___

Signature: Matt Green
Address: 716 Main, Nita City NT
Date: Oct 20, 19 YR-2 Occupation: Brakeman Age: 42

-119-
Fitzgerald Case File

SUPPLEMENT TO INCIDENT REPORT
10/26/YR-2

RE: Train XT471   From: Pat Rombach,
     Crossing #74647C   Investigator, N&W RR
     Rail-Highway

On October 20, YR-2, at approximately 6:00 pm, I was called to go to the subject crossing to investigate an incident. I arrived at approximately 6:20, briefly interviewed the train personnel and instructed the engineer and brakeman to write out their statements. I spoke with the state trooper (MIKE BENJAMIN #122) and reported to him that the train was traveling at approximately 48 m.p.h. per the engineer, confirmed by speed tape. I examined the train and the car wreckage, instructed the train crew to rerail the train and supervised the removal of the car from the tracks. I then examined the crossing, discovered two gouge marks near the tracks where the car had run into the train and also observed the condition of the crossing sign. Since it was after sunset, I felt that I could not take effective pictures of the scene that day. The trooper had taken some pictures that I felt would be useful.

I returned two days later, October 22, at 2:30 pm, to take photographs of the scene. Photos 7,8,9,10 and 11 are taken at eye level from a distance 50 feet west of the crossing. These pictures were taken in order to develop a panorama view of the crossing and tracks and to simulate what the driver would have seen at that distance. Photos 12, 13 and 14 were taken in the same fashion and with the same purpose at a distance of 75 feet west. Photos 15, 16 and 17 were also taken in the same manner and with the same purpose at a distance of 100 feet west. Photos 20 and 21 were taken from a point 200 feet west of the crossing in the same manner and with the same purpose; the tracks are clearly visible as is the crossing sign. The crossing sign was in adequate condition for its use but required some repair which I authorized. It was located at the north side of the tracks and had weathered lettering on both sides. I filed report 376 (REQUEST FOR EQUIPMENT INSTALLATION) on October 22. Coupled with the request was a suggestion to place a crossing sign on the south side of the road, facing west. I also examined the road to the west and found no advance warning sign on the road. I requested placement of a sign by the Douglas County authorities who have discretionary authority for such signage on October 22 using report 783 (ADVICE TO LOCAL HIGHWAY AUTHORITY).

I examined the records of the railroad and found only one prior incident at this crossing, which occurred in YR-15. Only minor property damage occurred when a farmer's pickup had been hit by a train at night after the truck had been stolen and left on the tracks.

On October 25, I contacted the brakeman to come to my office for a statement as to exactly what he saw. The brakeman submitted the statement.

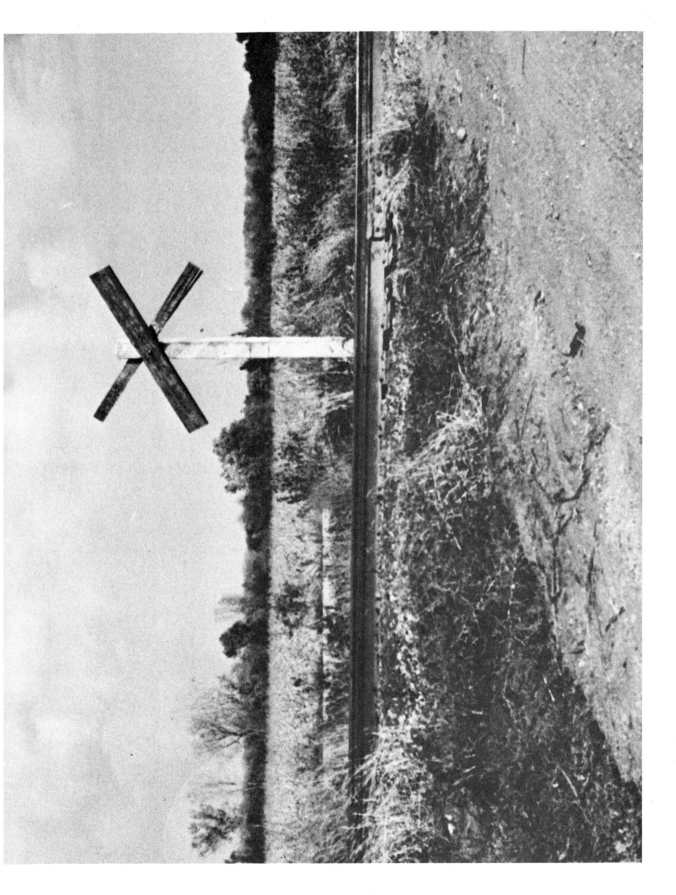

-133-
Fitzgerald Case File

Fitzgerald Case File

Fitzgerald Case File

Fitzgerald Case File

-149-
Fitzgerald Case File

STATEMENT

My name is Matt Green, age 42, married and I live at 716 Maine Street, Nita City. I am employed by the Nita and Western Railroad as a brakeman. I have been with the railroad for about 14 years. Before that I was a truck driver for the U.S. Army, serving in Germany.

On October 20, YR-2, I was working as a brakeman for the second engine (number 1964) on Train XT471, which is the local freight train from Lisle to Nita City. The engineer was Steve Smolen and the conductor in the first engine (number 1563) was Rich April. Our train consisted of four engines, followed by 85 cars (21 loaded, 64 empty) and had a total weight of 4033 tons. As we moved north on the single line track, we were traveling at approximately 48 miles per hour when we were hit by a car at crossing #74647C. I was seated in the second engine, left hand side. As we approached the crossing, we passed the whistle board and the whistle began to blow. I was looking left at an angle toward the road, because my responsibility is to look for oncoming traffic. At about 1200 feet away, I could see about 150 feet up the road, but could see more of the road as we got closer. At 350 feet from the crossing, growth and shrubbery on the road blocked my view of part of the road. There were weeds along the railroad right of way, but they did not block my view. Just before the crossing, I looked up the road and could see about 350 feet to the top of the hill, but could not see the road all of the way to the hilltop because the road dips. At no point did I see any cars coming.

It is also the brakeman's responsibility to look over the rear of the train when you have the opportunity. Since we were coming up on a curve, after the crossing I began to turn in my seat to look back at the train. I had my back to the side window at the time of the impact. I heard a sound like the shattering of glass and I looked out of the back window and saw rock and dirt flying. I only realized what had happened after the train had stopped. At the time of the collision I looked at the speed tape recorder, and it was showing 48 miles per hour.

After the train stopped, I went back along the train on the east side looking for whatever had caused the train to emergency. Rich April was on the west side. The first thing we saw was of course the remains of a car between the rails, after the first car and before the rest of the train. Then we started walking along the rest of the train and saying "here's another part of the car" until Rich found Mr. Fitzgerald. The trooper was on the scene by this time and I stayed to watch over the body until the mortuary arrived.

The weather was clear and dry, the gravel road was in good condition and the crossing was protected by a crossbuck sign.

At the time of the accident, I was seated 12 feet above the ground in the second engine. The measurements of the four engines and the box car are:

Unit 1 (#1563)	55 feet,	11 inches
Unit 2 (#1964)	56 feet,	2 inches
Unit 3 (#1560)	55 feet,	11 inches
Unit 4 (#1965)	56 feet,	2 inches
Box Car #1	44 feet,	4 inches

I have read this statement and it is correct to the best of my recollection and belief.

Matt Green
Matt Green

Signed at Nita City, Nita, on the 25th day of October, YR-2.

Witnessed: *Pat Rombach*
Pat Rombach
Investigator for N&W RR.

MEMORANDUM

TO: Cotton & McLeod, Attorneys
FROM: Pat Rombach, Investigator, Nita & Western RR
DATE: January 29, YR-1
SUBJECT: Incident of October 20, YR-2

At your request and instruction, I went to the scene of the incident on January 28 at 11:00 am to take further pictures of the scene and a simulated train.

Photos PR1 through PR8 were taken at a distance of 250 feet west of the crossing, looking east and observing a freight train with four pulling engines. The crossing is clearly visible as is the train. As you can see the crossing now contains two crossing signs. The four engines are of the same size and length as the train involved in this incident, as is the first box car.

Photo PR9 was taken 75 feet east of the tracks, looking west.

I was also asked to provide some background on myself. I have been employed by N&W for ten and a half years and have been serving as an investigator for the last eight years. I am 39 years old and worked as claims adjuster for an insurance company between high school and my coming to N&W.

Fitzgerald Case File

Fitzgerald Case File

Fitzgerald Case File

Fitzgerald Case File

DEPOSITION OF CAROL BUTTERFIELD*
MARCH 20, YR-1

My name is Carol Butterfield. I am 23 years and was born in Wellington, Nita on July 2, YR-25. I am married to Paul Butterfield and we live with our 9-month old daughter, Shelly, at 234 Deerfield in Marion, approximately 250 miles from Wellington. Both Paul and I grew up in Wellington, and Paul is two years older than me. Paul is employed at Acme Insurance as a claims adjuster and I am a housewife.

Paul, Johnny Fitzgerald and I were best friends, having grown up together and been classmates at school. In fact, Johnny was the best man at our wedding on July 4, YR-3. Johnny and I dated in high school, but I was more serious about him than he was about me. He began to date Debi and they got married real quick. I didn't get to see much of Johnny after that. I got to be friendly again with Johnny and met Debi when I started dating Paul about a year before our wedding and we really got close during a camping trip that summer. As a matter of fact, Johnny and I had a long talk about my marrying Paul, because I was afraid that it would affect his relationship with Paul. I still felt a lot for Johnny. I even kidded that we ought to sneak away that night and be together one last time before I told Paul I would marry him. Johnny said that my marriage to Paul would be the greatest thing that could happen to Paul and to not marry Paul would hurt Paul, and Johnny, very much.

After Paul and I got married and moved to Marion, we always tried to get together with the Fitzgeralds whenever we came to Wellington to visit Paul's mom and dad, Jeri and Al. I was a bit more friendly with Johnny than with Debi. For some reason, Debi was sometimes cool towards me. I think that she may have been jealous that Paul, Johnny and I had such a strong friendship and that we always kidded around so much. Debi was from Nita City and really didn't think much of people from the country. We did get along pretty well, though.

On October 19, YR-2, we traveled to Wellington with our new baby to visit with my in-laws and to help celebrate the birthday of one of our friends, George Carlisle. Johnny and Debi were going to stay over at the house that night. At

---

*The transcript of Carol Butterfield's deposition was excerpted so that only her answers are reprinted here. Assume that this is a true and accurate rendering of those answers.

DEPOSITION OF: CAROL BUTTERFIELD
DATE: MARCH 20, YR-1

about 5:30, the Fitzgeralds arrived and Johnny went downstairs to play pool with Paul, George and another friend, Richie. Debi and her 5 year old daughter, Carrie, were with me, my mother-in-law and my baby. I could tell that something was bothering Johnny and Debi because they seemed very quiet. The guys left about 8:00 to go to Rocco's for dinner and beer. Debi and I started to prepare the children's dinner. I had to go to the store for some diapers and I asked Debi if she wanted to go with me. We left in our car at about 8:45 to go to the store, which was about two blocks away. We got the diapers pretty quickly and came back into the house. We fed the children and put them to sleep. At about 9:30, we left in the car to go to Rocco's to meet the guys.

We got to Rocco's shortly thereafter and stayed for about 1 hour, having 2 beers each. I danced with Johnny for one dance and asked him what he wanted for his birthday. He said something like a new life, or something, and I asked him if there was anything wrong. He said that he wanted to talk and we went to a corner booth for a few minutes. He said that he and Debi were having a tough time. She had met a guy at her job that she had spent time with. She had packed clothes for herself and Carrie and she and Carrie were going to leave Johnny the next day to go to live at her parents' home for a while until they straightened things out. He really wanted to talk to Paul, but felt he really couldn't bring up the situation. He said that he really couldn't live without Debi and Carrie, and that maybe he should drive his car into a bridge to end it all but I felt that he really didn't mean it. He felt that Paul could really talk to Johnny and help him, but he really couldn't start the conversation. Needless to say, I was very surprised that Johnny was telling me this. I said let's wait until everyone comes home tonight and I will ask Paul if Johnny seemed okay and if he had noticed anything, then I would ask Paul to talk to Johnny before everyone left on Sunday. We then went back to our table.

At about 10:45 I called back to check on the baby. My mother-in-law told me the baby had just awakened and I decided to go home to nurse the baby. Debi and I left, but we didn't talk about Johnny during the ride. We went back to the house, and I nursed the baby and fell asleep. Debi stayed in the TV room alone. Some time later, I don't know exactly what time, Johnny helped Paul into our bedroom, because Paul had a little too much to drink. I was half asleep at the time and told Johnny we would see him in the morning.

DEPOSITION OF: CAROL BUTTERFIELD
DATE: MARCH 20, YR-1

The next morning I woke up about 5 am and found that Johnny and Debi's car was gone and their bed had not been slept in. I then went back to sleep. When I woke up again around 8:30, I asked Paul how he felt and if Johnny had said anything last night about any problems at home. Paul said that Johnny seemed a little moody but hadn't said anything specific. I then said that maybe he should call Johnny that day to see if everything was OK. I didn't want to tell Paul about what Johnny had told me, thinking that it should come from Johnny. Paul said he would call that afternoon, since he needed to talk to Johnny about the hunting they were going to do the following week. Paul went back to sleep.

At about 10:00, Debi called and my mother-in-law gave me the phone. Debi said goodbye and asked me to have Paul call Johnny before we left. I told her that Paul was going to call back later that day. She thanked us for being such good friends and hung up.

Paul tried to call Johnny at about 1:00 and then again at 3:00, thinking that Johnny would be watching the football game, but there was no answer. We tried again at 7:00, but again there was no answer. I then called Debi at her parents' house in Nita City to tell her that we hadn't talked to Johnny yet. Debi said she didn't know where Johnny would be, but to keep trying, that maybe he had just gone out for a pizza. At about 11:30, we got a phone call from Debi's mother, Mrs. Kay. She told me that they had gotten a phone call while Debi was at the laundromat that Johnny had been killed in a train accident. She had gone to the laundromat to tell her and Debi had fainted and they had to take her to the hospital. When Debi awoke, she told Mrs. Kay to call Paul and I to let us know what had happened. I gave Paul the bad news and also told him about what Johnny had told me about their family problems and Debi's leaving Johnny. Paul said no wonder Johnny killed himself.

Although Paul didn't want me to talk to Debi again, I spoke with her at the funeral on Wednesday. She told me "I don't know what I have done to deserve this, but whatever it was, it's too late now." We didn't talk any more because she started crying. Paul and I went back to Marion right after the funeral. Paul was really broken up. He had lost his best friend. He is still upset over the whole matter.

About a week after the funeral, my mother-in-law sent us a newspaper article written by Debi's mother. She wrote that Johnny's death was the railroad's fault. I guess she

DEPOSITION OF: CAROL BUTTERFIELD
DATE: MARCH 20, YR-1

couldn't believe that Johnny would kill himself. Under the circumstances, I guess that Johnny took the only way he thought he had.

    I have read this deposition and the answers are correct to the best of my knowledge and belief.

Carol Butterfield
Carol Butterfield
March 20, YR-1

Harold Bench
Notary Public

DEPOSITION OF PAUL BUTTERFIELD*
APRIL 28, YR-1

My name is Paul Butterfield. I am 25 years old and was born in Wellington, Nita on September 11, YR-27. I am married to Carol Butterfield and we have one daughter, Shelly. We live in Marion, Nita. I have agreed to give you lawyers this deposition over the telephone, but I will not sign anything and will not willingly testify in this case. I will not help Debi Fitzgerald in this lawsuit after what she did to Johnny, but I feel bad for Carrie also. The railroad is at fault also for not putting up automatic crossing gates at the crossing.

I knew Johnny Fitzgerald all my life. He was like a brother to me. We went through school together and spent most of our time together. He was the best friend a person could have. We always went hunting together every fall, in fact we were going hunting the week after he died. He was a great guy.

I know Debi Fitzgerald. She started to go out with Johnny in high school, although she was from Nita City. She and Johnny had met at a dance the summer of YR-8. Johnny had been dating Carol during the fall but he broke up with her when he started to date Debi. Debi got pregnant and they got married. I wasn't able to be at the wedding, because I was at a basketball tournament. Their daughter, Carrie, was born that spring. They seemed happy, but I guess you never really know.

I started to date Carol in the summer of YR-4. I didn't think that the fact that Johnny and Carol had dated was important and both Johnny and Carol felt the same way. We went camping that summer, the four of us, and really had a good time. I thought that any possible problems in our friendship with each other were eliminated when Carol agreed to marry me after the camping trip. We were married the next summer.

I remember the last visit we had with Johnny. We had come to Wellington to help celebrate a friend's birthday. Johnny and his family were going to spend the night at my

---

*The transcript of Paul Butterfield's deposition was excerpted so that only her answers are reprinted here. Assume that this is a true and accurate rendering of those answers.

DEPOSITION OF: PAUL BUTTERFIELD
DATE: APRIL 28, YR-1

parents' house. The guys were playing pool and then we went out for beers and food. Johnny seemed all right, but perhaps a little quiet. He was usually a pretty outgoing guy, but he just wasn't joking around too much that night. I talked with him about hunting on October 28, but he seemed pretty depressed and told me that he wanted to give me his favorite shotgun. I didn't understand then why he was acting this way and wanted to give me the shotgun, but I guess I now know why. I had a little too much beer and Johnny carried me home. I thought he was going to stay overnight, but he was gone the next morning. My wife asked me if I thought everything was OK with Johnny and I said that Johnny was acting kind of moody but that I would call him later to check up on him.

I tried to call Johnny all afternoon, but got no answer. At 7:00, Carol called Debi at her mother's house to see if Johnny was there, but he wasn't. I kept on calling until about 10:00. At about 11:30, the phone rang and Carol spoke. She came into the living room and told me that Johnny was dead. She also told me what Johnny had told her the night before about Debi and that guy. Johnny was a careful driver. He wouldn't have driven onto a crossing if he knew the train was coming unless he wanted to kill himself. There's no doubt in my mind that if Johnny knew he was going to lose Debi and Carrie that he would choose not to live. I just wish he would have talked to me about the situation. Maybe I could have talked him out of it. Maybe I could have talked to Debi. Maybe I could have done something.

I don't want to have anything to do with Debi Fitzgerald and I don't want my wife to, either. If she agrees to testify that's her business, but I will not. I just hope that if Debi gets any money from this lawsuit that some of it goes to Carrie and not Debi and her mother. That's all I have to say.

It is hereby stipulated and agreed by and between the counsel for the respective parties that the reading and signing of the deposition by the witness are expressly waived by counsel and the witness and all objections are preserved until the time of trial.

DEPOSITION OF: PAUL BUTTERFIELD
DATE: APRIL 28, YR-1

I, Harold Bench, Notary Public and Court Reporter for the State of Nita, do certify that this deposition was taken telephonically, that Paul Butterfield was sworn by me to tell the truth and that his deposition was reduced to writing by me.

Harold Bench
Harold Bench

Dated: April 28, YR-1

DEPOSITION OF JERI BUTTERFIELD*
APRIL 14, YR-1

My name is Jeri Butterfield. I am 51 years old and my birthdate is May 26, YR-52. I live at 905 Holiday in Wellington, Nita with my husband, Al.

Yes, I did know Johnny Fitzgerald. Johnny was a friend of my son, Paul Butterfield, who will be 26 on September 11, throughout high school and in fact was my son's best man at Paul's wedding, which was on July 4, YR-3. During the wedding, I had an opportunity to talk with Johnny and he told me how happy he was, having found the girl of his dreams and, now with a daughter, he had lots to live for and really had it made.

On Friday, October 18, YR-2 my son and his wife, Carol, and their 4-month old baby girl, Shelly, came to visit us from their home in Marion. They also came to help celebrate the birthday of George Carlisle, a high school friend of Paul and Johnny.

On Saturday, Johnny and his wife, Debi, and 5-year old daughter, Carrie, came to our house to see my son and his family. They were going to spend the night with us in the guest room downstairs. Everyone seemed to be in good spirits. At about 6:00 p.m., Johnny, Paul, George and another friend, Richie, were in our basement playing pool, while Carol, Debi and the children were upstairs watching television with me and my husband. At about 8:00 pm, the boys decided to go out for some dinner and beers at Rocco's, a bar about five blocks away. At about 8:45 pm, Carol and Debi went out to get some diapers for Carol's baby. I know it was right before 9 because the store closes at 9. The store is about two blocks away. They came back in about 15 minutes, just after 9. Then Carol and Debi fed their daughters and decided to go up to Rocco's to meet the boys. They left about 9:30.

Carol called at about 10:45 pm to ask about the baby, just as the baby woke up. I told her the baby was up and she and Debi came home, getting in about 11:00. I went to sleep at 11:30, before the boys had come home and I didn't hear them come home.

---

*The transcript of Jeri Butterfield's deposition was excerpted so that only her answers are reprinted here. Assume that this is a true and accurate rendering of those answers.

DEPOSITION OF: JERI BUTTERFIELD
DATE: APRIL 14, YR-1

When I woke up the next morning, Johnny and his family were gone and their beds were not slept in. Carol woke up and joined me in the kitchen. At about 10:00 am, the phone rang. It was Debi and she asked for Carol. They talked about five minutes, but I don't know what it was about.

Paul tried to call Johnny a few times during the afternoon. He said he wanted to check with Johnny about some good places for hunting that Johnny was going to look for. They were to go hunting the next week. He also said he wanted to check up on Johnny, but I wasn't sure what he meant by that.

At 11:30 pm that evening, the phone rang and woke me up. It was Debi's mother, Ethel Kay, asking to talk to Carol or Paul. I said that they were asleep and she said to tell Paul and Carol that Johnny had died in a car accident, I was totally shocked. At this point, Carol came into the room and talked with Debi's mother.

A week or so after the funeral, I read a letter to the editor in the newspaper from Debi's mother, Ethel Kay. It said that the railroad was negligent in not making sure that the crossing was upgraded with flashing signals and bells, that someone had died and with the increased use of the road, more people would die. I clipped out the letter and sent it to my son and daughter-in-law.

A few weeks ago, Carol called and told me she had given a deposition to the lawyers and was concerned about what was going on. I called Debi's mother and told her that Carol didn't want to hurt Debi or Carrie and she said if Carol didn't want to hurt them she should stay out of it.

My son is still sad about losing Johnny and has said that he lost the best friend he ever had, just like losing a brother.

I have read this deposition and the answers are correct to the best of my knowledge and belief.

Jeri Butterfield
Jeri Butterfield
April 14, YR-1

Harold Borch
Notary Public

DEPOSITION OF NICK BARON*
JUNE 22, YR-1

My name is Nick Baron. I live at 9225 Indian Creek Parkway, Nita City. I am 66 years old and retired. For the period September, YR-3, until January, YR-1, I was supervisor of welders at the Uprite Scaffolding plant in Wellington. As supervisor, it was my job to organize work schedules and make sure that my workers were doing their job.

I was Johnny Fitzgerald's supervisor at the plant. Before the plant opened, I knew Johnny from the old plant but did not come into regular contact with him. After we were both transferred to the new plant, we talked about scheduling. Johnny had requested the seven-to-three shift so that he could spend time with his daughter after he came home from work. Since he was a good worker, I agreed to his request.

Beginning in August, YR-2, Johnny's work habits became a little strange. Although he never came to work late before, he was late for work four times between September 15 and the date he died (October 20, YR-2). The last time he was late, I thought I smelled alcohol on his breath, but Johnny said it was mouthwash. He explained that the reason he had been late recently was because his daughter had been ill and he needed to help take care of her in the mornings.

During the last month, he seemed a little distant and was not as outgoing as before, but I didn't think anything of it at the time. Everyone gets like that sometimes.

I used to live near the plant in Wellington. Before it was built, the only people who drove out in that area were people who lived out there and hunters. During construction, the crews started going out there more and once the plant opened, the roads got well travelled. Uprite employed 750 people at the plant for the day shift and 250 for the night shift. Sometimes I travelled on County Road across the tracks, but I never was there when the train crossed.

I was sorry to hear about Johnny's death. He was a nice person.

---

*The transcript of Nick Baron's deposition was excerpted so that only her answers are reprinted here. Assume that this is a true and accurate rendering of those answers.

DEPOSITION OF: NICK BARON
DATE: JUNE 22, YR-1

    I have read this deposition and the answers are correct to the best of my knowledge and belief.

                                                               Nick Baron

Notary Public

JOSHUA ALAN

CONSULTING ENGINEER

Redmond Road   Nita City, Nita

May 21, YR-1

John Cotton, Esq.   RE: Fitzgerald v. Nita &
Cotton & McLeod   Western Railroad
Regency Plaza
Suite 1300
Nita City, Nita

Dear John:

In connection with your request to examine the above mentioned matter, I have had the opportunity to study the police report and the report compiled by the Nita & Western investigator, including the photos. I am especially impressed with the photo and description of the marks at the scene described by the trooper. In addition, I have today examined the scene of the collision.

Based upon the reports, photographs and my examination, I have determined that the coefficient of friction for the surface of the road and the tires on the car was between .46 and .52. Using this coefficient of friction, and based upon an estimated speed of the car at the maximum speed limit of 50 miles per hour, Mr. Fitzgerald's car should have left between 155 and 180 feet of skid marks. Assuming that it took between one-half and one second to react to the train (a reasonable reaction time), Mr. Fitzgerald's car would have travelled 37 to 74 feet before the brakes locked the wheels. These figures show that Mr. Fitzgerald had enough time to see the train, react and apply his brakes in sufficient time to prevent the collision. Accordingly, in my opinion the railroad's maintenance of the foliage along the roadway was reasonable.

Based upon my experience in the field, the tests I have conducted on other cars and roads as well as the information referred to above, it is my opinion that the marks on the road that were present at the time of the collision were a result of the car being dragged by the train upon impact. The marks were not skid marks. Indeed, there is no evidence that Mr. Fitzgerald ever applied his brakes. If there was an attempt to stop the car with the associated locking of brakes, then skid marks would have been in evidence.

Based upon the four hours I spent in this investigation, my charge for this report is $160.00. Thank you for the opportunity to consult on this matter.

Sincerely,

Joshua Alan

Nita State Police, Nita City, NT

DISTANCE (feet)	SPEED (mph)	COEFFICIENT OF FRICTION
200, 180, 160, 140, 120, 110, 100, 90, 80, 70, 60, 50, 40, 30, 25, 20, 15, 10	100, 90, 80, 70, 60, 50, 40, 35, 30, 25, 20, 15, 10, 5	120, 110, 100, 90, 80, 70, 60, 50, 40, 35, 30, 25, 20, 15, 10, 9

HOW TO ESTIMATE SPEED FROM SKIDMARKS: Draw a straight line from the coefficient of friction (from chart on other side) to the average accident skidmark length.

FOR BIAS-PLY TIRES ONLY

COEFFICIENT OF FRICTION: Application for passenger cars and light duty trucks with normal tire wear on relatively flat roads.

ROAD CONDITION	COEFFICIENT
New asphalt, dry	85
New asphalt, wet	80
New concrete, dry	78
New concrete, wet	74
Old concrete, dry	63
Good gravel, wet	60
Old concrete, wet	56
Old asphalt, dry	55
Old asphalt, wet	53
Good gravel, dry	52
Loose gravel, wet or dry	46
Tarred dirt, dry	40
Dirt, dry	36
Mud	28
Tarred dirt, wet	22
Packed snow (no chains)	20
Smooth ice (no chains)	9

If the vehicle has stopped on a hill, or has excessively worn tires, or if the pavement conditions changed over the course of bringing the vehicle to a stop, this chart may not be used.

DEPOSITION OF STEVE SMOLEN*
MARCH 19, YR-1

My name is Steve Smolen. I am 38 years old and was born in Nita City on June 25, YR-40. I live at 449 Clearmeadow in Nita City. I am an engineer with the Nita and Western Railroad and have been with them for 10 years. I worked for the Louisville & Nashville Railroad for 10 years before that.

I am familiar with the crossing where the accident occurred, having been on the run for 7 years. I go over that crossing five to six times each week. The crossing was protected by one crossbuck, on the eastern side. At the time of the collision, I thought it was a "farmer's crossing" meaning a private road going to a farmhouse. No one at N & W ever told me that it was a county road crossing.

On October 20, YR-2, I was the engineer on Train XT471 running from Lisle to Nita City. The train had four engines and 85 cars. The weather was clear and dry, although it was beginning to get dusky as it was getting closer to sundown. I was in the lead engine on the right side. Rich April was the conductor and he was on the left side of the lead engine. Matt Green was the brakeman in the second engine. We got to the crossing about 5:45 p.m. About a quarter of a mile south of the crossing we passed a whistle board, which signifies the beginning of a whistle sequence. I began to blow the whistle, two longs, a short and a long, repeated. There was nothing unusual during the crossing. After we passed about 5 car lengths after the crossing, I started losing air on the engine, indicating that there was a break in the air line and the brakes started setting up. I got the train to a complete stop and got out of the engine to look for the problem. The wheels on the box car were sideways on the track and I saw what was left of a car on the tracks south of the engine portion of the train. The rest of the train was beyond the auto to the south. It had separated the boxes from the engines after the first box.

At the time of the collision, the whistle was blowing and the headlight was on. It was beginning to get dark, but was still pretty light out. We were traveling about 45-50

---

*The transcript of Steve Smolen's deposition was excerpted so that only her answers are reprinted here. Assume that this is a true and accurate rendering of those answers.

DEPOSITION OF: STEVE SMOLEN
DATE: MARCH 19, YR-1

miles per hour and at that speed it took me at least three-quarters of a mile to stop the train. There was no speed recorder and tape in the lead engine. I didn't know there was one in the second engine, but I now know that there was.

After the collision, Pat Rombach, the N & W investigator came to the site to collect our written reports and handle the matters with the trooper. We reattached the train at about 7:00 pm and continued on our route.

I was on the same track a few days later and noticed that the railroad had placed another crossbuck on the west side of the crossing.

During the period before the collision, I did not notice any appreciable increase in the number of cars crossing there. We usually came by at 5:15-6:00 in the evening and rarely saw any traffic there, especially on a Sunday.

I have read this deposition and the answers are correct to the best of my knowledge and belief.

_____
Steve Smolen

_____
Notary Public

MEMORANDUM

TO: Rich McLeod, John Cotton
FROM: Dave Didion, Paralegal
DATE: August 24, YR-1
SUBJECT: Interview with our Economist

At your request, I submitted the Plaintiffs' economist's report to our expert, Prof. Gary Mason, Chairman of the Economics Department at Nita State University. He examined the report and has advised me of the following suggested points for criticism.

1. Gelber assumes that the fringe benefits were standard and uses a national study to arrive at figure of 20.63% of gross income. Firstly, this figure may in fact be less; Gelber did not make any attempt to discover the actual numbers. They may be higher, but probably are lower. Mason did not look at the actual figures either, but the figure for other industries in the Wellington is in the range of 16-20%. Nonetheless, the fringe benefits are not really a loss to the survivors. Fringe benefits are personal to the employee and are difficult to transfer to another person. With the exception of dependent medical coverage, all other benefits are things that the survivors could not have enjoyed during Fitzgerald's lifetime and the loss of which is not something for which they should be compensated at all.

2. Gelber uses national unemployment rates for white males as a group, but again has not examined the rates for the industry and locality. Mason's figures range from .5 to 2.0% higher for the unemployment in the Wellington/Nita City area. My sources at the Uprite plant indicate that they are about to begin a massive layoff at the plant with everyone who has been there eight years or less being furloughed for at least one year.

3. Gelber bases his value of the loss of household services on an increase in the amount of services as the person gets older. In fact, people tend to do less and contract more as they get older. Therefore, this figure is overstated. Moreover, the figures are projected to increase at almost 6%, a figure which is higher than Gelber's projected increase rate in wages. Gelber appears to be saying that the decedent's time is more valuable doing household work rather than regular employment. On the other hand, Gelber uses figures for a husband with a working spouse, and this

might not necessarily be the case. Gelber has also not taken into account the possible remarriage of Mrs. Fitzgerald; this would negate any necessary recovery for household services as a new husband would perform the services that the decedent would have done.

4. Gelber uses a personal consumption rate of 35-49% and has again based a valuable piece of information on national standards rather than actual information. If there was a history of higher consumption, such as expensive hobbies, drinking, gambling, travel or the like than the number subtracted would be higher, and the resulting loss would be lower.

5. Gelber has projected an increase in wages at 5.4% per year. Mason indicates that the wages at the Uprite plant, which is non-union, has averaged only 3.9% over the last 3 years. The plant has a good chance of going union this year, and the rates may be in the area of 6-7% for the next few years.

6. Gelber has projected a rate of return on investment at 7.5%. This figure is realistic, but greater rates of return on nongovernment investment opportunities are available in the 10% range. While these investments are not guaranteed or "risk-free", the risk may be spread such that they are really at no risk.

7. Obviously, Gelber has not considered the issues of suicide or the imminent breakup of the family in reaching his conclusions. Mason's guess is that Gelber wasn't told of these factors, but that they might not change any of Gelber's opinions. Indeed, in a family separation case, child support/alimony payments may be more constant. They would also not be more than 40% of gross income, even with the increases projected by Gelber over the years. Thus 40% of the present value of the loss in wages and fringes would only be $201,100.

APPLICABLE NITA STATUTES

Motor Vehicles-Chapter 89

Section 71. Obedience to signal indicating approach of train. (a). Whenever any person dirving a vehicle approaches a railroad crossing under any of the circumstances stated in this section, the driver of such vehicle shall stop within fifty (50) feet but not less than fifteen (15) feet from the nearest rail of such railroad, and shall not proceed until he or she can do so safely. The foregoing requirements shall apply when:
  (1). A clearly visible electric or mechanical signal device gives warning of the immediate approach of a railroad train;
  (2). A crossing gate is lowered or when a human flagman gives or continues to give a signal of the approach or passage of a railroad train;
  (3) A railroad train approaching within approximately one thousand two hundred (1200) feet of the highway crossing emits a signal audible from such distance and such railroad train, by reason of its speed or nearness to such crossing, is an immediate hazard; or
  (4) An approaching railroad train is plainly visible and is in hazardous proximity to such crossing.

Public Utilities-Chapter 66

Section 120. Failure of locomotive to sound whistle at crossing. An air whistle shall be attached to each locomotive engine, and shall be sounded four (4) times (two long, one short, one log) beginning at least 1200 feet from where the railroad shall cross any public road and shall be repeated until the crossing is occupied by the engine, under penalty of a fine of $20.00 for every neglect of the provisions of this section.

Section 212. Duty to maintain foliage at crossings. All railroads shall maintain the foliage along roads which intersect railroad tracks by mowing and clearing sufficiently to permit a motorist to observe an oncoming train from a distance appropriate to the allowable speed of the roadway.

Wrongful Death-Chapter 70.

Section 1. Liability. Whenever the death of a person shall be caused by wrongful act, neglect, or default, and the act, neglect, or default is such as would, if death had not ensued, have entitled the party injured to maintain an action and recover damages in respect thereof, then, and in every such case, the person who or company or corporation which would have been liable if death had not ensued, shall be liable to an action for damages, notwithstanding the death of the person injured, and although the death shall have been caused under such circumstances as amount in law to a felony.

Section 2. Damages.

A. Damages recoverable for death by wrongful act include:

(1) Expenses for care, treatment, and hospitalization incident to the injury resulting in death;

(2) Compensation for pain and suffering of the decedent;

(3) The reasonable funeral expenses of the decedent;

(4) The present monetary value of the decedent to the persons entitled to receive the damages recovered, including but not limited to compensation for the loss of the reasonable expected;

    (a) net income of the decedent,
    (b) services, protection, care, and assistance of the decedent, whether voluntary or obligatory, to the persons entitled to the damages recovered,
    (c) society, companionship, comfort, guidance, kindly offices, and advice of the decedent to the persons entitled to the damages recovered;

(5) Such punitive damages as the decedent could have recovered had he or she survived, and the punitive damages for wrongfully causing the death of the decedent through maliciousness, willful or wanton injury, or gross negligence;

(6) Nominal damages when the jury so finds.

B. All evidence which reasonably tends to establish any of the elements of damages included in subsection A, or otherwise reasonably tends to establish the present monetary value of the decedent to the persons entitled to receive the damages recovered, is admissible in an action for damages for death by wrongful act.

Comparative Negligence-Chapter 140

    Section 3. Contributory Negligence No Bar to Recovery of Damages. In all actions hereafter brought for personal injuries, or where such injuries have resulted in death, or for injury to property, the fact that the person injured, or the owner of the property, or the person having control over the property may have been guilty of contributory negligence shall not bar a recovery, but damages shall be diminished by the jury in proportion to the amount of negligence attributable to the person injured, or the owner of the property, or the person having control over the property.

Fitzgerald Case File

PROPOSED JURY INSTRUCTIONS

1. The Court will now instruct you on the claims and defenses of each party and the law that will apply to the case. You must arrive at your verdict by applying the law as you now receive it to the facts of the case.

2. The parties to this case are Debra Fitzgerald, on her own behalf, as the mother of Carrie Fitzgerald and as the administrator of the Estate of Johnny Fitzgerald, as plaintiffs, and the Nita & Western Railroad Co., as defendant.

3. Defendant has admitted in the pleadings, and you must regard as conclusively proven the following:

On October 20, YR-2, Johnny Fitzgerald was operating his car on County Road in Douglas County, Nita, traveling easterly and approaching Nita & Western rail crossing #74647C. At the intersection of County Road and the Nita & Western tracks Johnny Fitzgerald's car and the Nita & Western train collided. Johnny Fitzgerald died as a result of injuries sustained in the collision. On November 15, YR-2, Debra Fitzgerald was appointed the administratrix of the Estate of Johnny Fitzgerald. Johnny Fitzgerald was survived by Debra Fitzgerald, his wife, and by Carrie Fitzgerald, his daughter.

4. Plaintiffs claim that Nita & Western was negligent in its operation of the train or by its failure to warn Johnny Fitzgerald of the oncoming train, and that its negligence caused Johnny Fitzgerald's injuries and death. Plaintiffs seek damages for defendant's negligence on behalf of herself individually, her daughter and the estate. Defendant denies that Nita & Western was negligent and claims that Johnny Fitzgerald was either negligent or that he intentionally drove his car into the train, causing his injuries and death.

5. In this case, plaintiffs have the burden of proving that Nita & Western was negligent by:

   1. operating the train at an unsafe speed; or

   2. failing to keep an adequate lookout; or

   3. failing to sound its whistle and shine its headlamp; or

   4. failing to adequately notify that a crossing was present and a train was coming;

and that any such negligence was a proximate cause of Johnny Fitzgerald's death.

6. The defendant has the burden of proving that Johnny Fitzgerald was negligent in failing to maintain a proper lookout or that Johnny Fitzgerald intentionally took his own life and that such failure or intentional acts were a proximate cause of his death.

7. Thus each of the parties have a burden of proof to maintain, and you are to determine whether they have met their burdens. Your task is to determine whether Johnny Fitzgerald or the Nita & Western Railroad, or both of them, were negligent and the extent to which their respective negligence caused the death of Johnny Fitzgerald or whether Johnny Fitzgerald committed suicide.

8. The terms "negligence" or "negligent" as used in these instructions mean the failure to use that degree of care that an ordinarily prudent person would use under the same or similar circumstances.

9. The term "contributory negligence" or "contributorily negligent" means negligence on the part of Johnny Fitzgerald.

10. Violations of a statute of the state of Nita, if you find such violations, are negligence as a matter of law. Such negligence has the same effect as any other acts of negligence.

11. It is the duty of a railroad company to use such care and precaution as ordinary prudence dictates. It must exercise greater care and vigilance in areas of more frequent crossings than in areas of less frequent crossings. The degree of care which the law requires to be exercised must be commensurate with the probability of danger. The railway crew must maintain a proper outlook and maintain proper control of the train. Proper lookout and control are such lookout and control as will avoid collision with cars being operated without negligence. While maintaining a lookout, the crew may assume that a driver of a car will bring the car to a stop until such time as it becomes apparent that the driver is not going to stop.

12. A statute of the state of Nita requires that an air whistle of a train be sounded at least 1200 feet from a railroad crossing and continue until the engine crosses the roadway, and shall consist of four sounds: two longs, one short and then one long.

13. A statute of the state of Nita provides that it is the duty of a railroad company to maintain the foliage along roads which intersect railroad tracks by mowing and clearing

sufficiently to permit a motorist traveling along the road to observe a train approaching the crossing from a distance appropriate to the allowable speed of the roadway.

14. It is the duty of the driver of a car to keep a proper lookout and have his car under proper control to avoid collisions or accidents, assuming other drivers are exercising ordinary care.

15. A statute of the state of Nita requires that a driver of a car approaching a railroad crossing shall stop at least 15 feet before the crossing, and not proceed until he can do so safely under the following circumstances:

   1. A railroad train approaching the crossing emits an audible sound within 1200 feet of the crossing and the train by reason of its speed or nearness is an immediate hazard; or

   2. An approaching train is clearly visible and is in hazardous proximity to the crossing.

16. It is the duty of a driver approaching a railroad crossing to look and listen at a time and place where looking and listening would be effective. Failure of the railroad to give signals at a railroad crossing does not relieve one about to cross a crossing from the duty to use due care to look and listen for an approaching train.

17. In a death action, where there is no direct evidence as to an accident causing fatal injury, facts and circumstances may be proven by circumstantial evidence. Unless the defendant establishes to the contrary by a preponderance of the evidence, the law requires you to assume that the instincts of natural love of life and hesitancy to die prevailed in the mind of Johnny Fitzgerald just prior to his death. If the preponderance of the evidence is that the death of Johnny Fitzgerald was attributable to his intentional act or omission, undertaken with an intent to commit suicide, then you are instructed to indicate this finding.

18. Proximate cause is that cause which, in the natural and continuous sequence, produces the injury, and without which the injury would not have occurred. To be a proximate cause of Johnny Fitzgerald's death, negligent conduct on the part of Johnny Fitzgerald or Nita & Western need not be the only cause, nor the last cause. It is sufficient if the negligent conduct acting concurrently with another cause produced the injury. Thus, there need not be only one proximate cause.

19. In the state of Nita, we have what is called a "pure comparative negligence" statute. The law provides that:

> In all actions hereafter brought for personal injuries, or where such injuries have resulted in death,. . . . the fact that the person injured . . . may have been guilty of contributory negligence shall not bar a recovery, but damages shall be diminished by the jury in proportion to the amount of negligence attributable to the person injured.

What this means is that the contributory negligence of Johnny Fitzgerald, if any, would not bar the plaintiff's recovery. The law directs you to apportion the responsibility and, thus, the damages in accordance with the relative fault of the parties. Therefore, the damages allowed to be recovered by the plaintiffs should be diminished in proportion to the amount of negligence which was a legal cause of the deceased's death and which was attributable to the deceased, whether or not such negligence is greater than that of the defendant.

20. You are to determine the negligence, if any, of both Johnny Fitzgerald and Nita & Western Railroad, and then to apportion the responsibility of each. Please state your findings of negligence in the following form:

We find the conduct of the defendant, Nita & Western Railroad, was _____ % percent negligent.

We find the conduct of the deceased, Johnny Fitzgerald, was _____ % percent negligent. The percentages must total 100%.

21. In this case you must also decide the issue of damages. You must determine the amount of damages which will reasonably and fairly compensate Debra Fitzgerald and Carrie Fitzgerald for the losses resulting from the death of Johnny Fitzgerald. In determining the loss, you should consider the following factors:

1. The reasonable funeral expenses of the decedent;

2. The present monetary value of the decedent to the persons entitled to receive damages recovered, including but not limited to, compensation for the loss of the reasonably expected;

   (a) net income of the decedent;

(b) services, protection, care, and assistance of the decedent, whether voluntary or obligatory, to the persons entitled to the damages recovered;

(c) society, companionship, comfort, guidance, kindly offices, and advice of the decedent to the persons entitled to the damages recovered;

3. Such punitive damages for wrongfully causing the death of the decedent through maliciousness, willful or wanton injury, or gross negligence;

4. Nominal damages when the jury so finds.

22. In determining the amount of damages to the plaintiffs you may consider how long the decedent was likely to have lived, that some persons work all their lives and that others do not, and that a person's earnings may remain the same, increase or decrease in the future.

IN THE CIRCUIT COURT OF
DOUGLAS COUNTY, NITA
CIVIL DIVISION

DEBRA FITZGERALD,   )
Administratrix of the Estate   )
of JOHNNY FITZGERALD, and   )
DEBRA FITZGERALD, individually   )
and on behalf of her minor child   )
CARRIE FITZGERALD   )
)
        Plaintiffs   )
)
    vs.   )   VERDICT
)
NITA & WESTERN RAILROAD CO.   )
)
        Defendant   )

The jury is to answer the following questions. The foreperson is to answer the questions for the jury and sign the verdict.

1. Was the death of Johnny Fitzgerald attributable to his intentional act or omission, undertaken with an intent to commit suicide?

        YES _____   NO _____

If your answer to question 1 is Yes, you need not continue your deliberations and should return to Court.

2. Do you find that either Johnny Fitzgerald or the Nita & Western Railroad were negligent?

        YES _____   NO _____

If your answer to question 2 is No, you need not continue your deliberations and should return to Court.

3. Please state your findings of negligence in the following form:

We find the conduct of the defendant, Nita & Western Railroad, was _____ % negligent.

We find the conduct of the deceased, Johnny Fitzgerald, was _____ % negligent.

The percentages must total 100%.

4. Please determine the total amount of damages to the plaintiffs, without regard to the amount of negligence attributable to either party.

_____

The Court will multiply the percentage of negligence that you find to be apportioned to the defendant, Nita & Western Railroad (question 3), by the amount of total damages you have determined (question 4), and that amount shall be the verdict for the plaintiffs.

_____
                                              Foreperson